Victorian Furniture

Book III

Styles and Prices

Robert and Harriett Swedberg

Other books by Robert W. and
Harriett Swedberg

Off Your Rocker
Victorian Furniture Styles and Prices, Revised
Victorian Furniture Styles and Prices, Book II
Country Pine Furniture Styles and Prices
American Oak Furniture Styles and Prices
Wicker Furniture Styles and Prices
Country Furniture and Accessories with Prices
American Oak Furniture Styles and Prices,
  Book II
Country Furniture and Accessories with Prices,
  Book II
Tins 'N' Bins
The Country Store 'N' More

On the Cover: Courtesy of the Terrace Hill Society, a view of the drawing room and music room at Terrace Hill, official residence of the governor of Iowa.

Cover and Book Design: Ann Eastburn
All Other Photography by the Authors
Printing and Enlarging by Tom Luse

Library of Congress Catalog
Card Number 79-101790

ISBN 0-87069-396-4

10 9 8 7 6 5 4 3 2 1

Published by

Wallace-Homestead Book Company
580 Waters Edge
Lombard, Illinois 60148

One of the *ABC PUBLISHING* ⓐⓑⓒ Companies

❧ Contents ❧

❧ Acknowledgments ❧

The authors sincerely thank the following collectors and dealers who gave freely of their time and knowledge to assist us in obtaining photographs and prices for this book. We also thank those who did not wish to be acknowledged individually.

ABC Antique Shoppe
West Des Moines, Iowa

Antique Scene
Rachel Cattrell
Moline, Illinois

Antiques, Art 'N Treasures
Steve and Virginia Hallett
Janesville, Wisconsin

Antiqueland Mall
Anthony and Jennifer Orton
Madison, Alabama

Charlie Apperson
Antiqueland Mall
Madison, Alabama

Annie Claire Atkinson

Banowetz Antiques
Virl and Kathy Banowetz
Maquoketa, Iowa

Beaumont House Antiques
Jim and Fawna Radewan
Rochester, Wisconsin

Bob's Antiques
Bob M. DeBerry
Whitewright, Texas

Brick House Antiques
Don and Liz Juhl
Waverly, Iowa

Brouwers Antiques
Bert Brouwer
Cross Plains, Wisconsin

Buttermilk Hill Antiques
Terry and Evangeline Husk
Franklin, Pennsylvania

Larry Carrier, Charles Lohr, and Bruce Rosenwasser
Rocky's Antique Mall
Weyer's Cave, Virginia

Cats 'N Dogs Antiques
John and Norman Beecher
West Branch, Iowa

Chalice Antique Shoppe
Skip and Mary Jane Hastings
Mt. Olive, Illinois

Cherokee Antiques
Larry and Cricket Hammond
Rocky's Antique Mall
Weyer's Cave, Virginia

Chic Antiques
Columbia Antique Mall
Columbia, South Carolina

Chris' Antiques — Quality Victorian
Lee and Chris Christenson
Urbana, Illinois

Churchmouse Antiques
Marilyn Johnson
Lawton, Michigan

Coach House Antiques
Ruth Fischer
New Market, Maryland

Bill and Margaret Collins

Country Collectibles
Joan W. McCall
Kent, Connecticut

Country Lane Antiques
Bill and Helen Oxenrider
Pierceton, Indiana

Country Treasures
Dick and Doris Thompson
Keokuk, Iowa

Mary Davin's Antiques
Iowa City, Iowa

Day's Past Antiques
Gary E. Hale
Breese, Illinois

Dim Lantern Antiques
Arlene Harrington
Franklin, Pennsylvania

Mr. and Mrs. Edward Gabrys

Gallery of the Three Associates
Peggy and Bob Miller
Antiqueland Mall
Madison, Alabama

Garland's Antiques
Garland Miller
Rocky's Antique Mall
Weyer's Cave, Virginia

Ralph and Virginia Gauze

Mr. and Mrs. Samuel Geake

The Grainery Antiques
Shirley and Syd Waggoner
Fort Wayne, Indiana

Joe and Beverly Hancock

Reverend and Mrs. E. W. Hancock

Terry Harper, Bookseller
Rouseville, Pennsylvania

Patricia Hayes Antiques
Bittersweet Shop
Gaylordsville, Connecticut

Hearn House Antiques
Antiqueland Mall
Madison, Alabama

The Helpers
Roger and Milly Ratcliff
Newton, Iowa

J. O. Hendrix Antiques
Columbia Antique Mall
Columbia, South Carolina

Marjorie Herman

Hillside Antiques
Estelle Holloway
Frankfort, Illinois

Charles Holland
Antiqueland Mall
Madison, Alabama

House of Stuff 'N Things
Anna Figg
Buffalo, Iowa

J's Antiques
Joe and Wanda Ackley
Lewisville, Texas

Dr. and Mrs. James O. Jensen

Brandon Jones
Antiqueland Mall
Madison, Alabama

Ken's Antiques and Collectibles
Kenneth Kite
Rocky's Antique Mall
Weyer's Cave, Virginia

Mona and Marc Klarman

LaMere Brightview
Moline, Illinois

Darlene and Walter Laud

Lionwood Antiques
Charles W. Hilliard
Bath, Ohio

Sam and Lawanna McClure

W. D. McDonald
Columbia Antique Mall
Columbia, South Carolina

Kitty and Carl Marshall

Mary Rachel Antique Shop
Mary Levery
Washington, Illinois

Alberta and Dick Medd

Miska's Antique Workshop
Joe Miska
Stanton, Virginia

Mockingbird Hill Antiques
Lee and Sara Rhoads
Lisbon, Iowa

Murphy's Antiques
Pat and Patsy
Whitewright, Texas

Nana's Front Room Antiques
Kathleen Constable
New Market, Maryland

Dr. and Mrs. Robert A. Nelson

Reverend and Mrs. Joe Newby

Odds & Ends Antiques
Wayne and Lida Hale
Vandalia, Illinois

The Oldest Son's Antiques and Appraisal Service
Jerry Nance
Pochahontas, Illinois

Sharon and Dick Olson

Pick's Antiques
Allen Edwards and Loren Randle
Chillicothe, Illinois

Plain and Fancy Antiques
Mildred M. Bark
Franklin, Pennsylvania

Pot Luck Antiques
Mrs. Jack Cunningham
Texarkana, Texas

Price Antiques
Lucille and David Price
Antiqueland Mall
Madison, Alabama

Clyde Rabon
Columbia Antique Mall
Columbia, South Carolina

Jeff Ramina Antiques
Jeff and Dolores
Baltimore, Maryland

Red Apple Antiques
Don and Alice Strube
Milwaukee, Wisconsin

Red Barn Antiques
Rhea Heppner
Chippewa Falls, Wisconsin

Ricklef's Antiques
Eloise and Doug
Anamosa, Iowa

Robbie's Antiques
Earle and Betty Robison
Lewisburg, Ohio

Jack and Bonnie Roberts

Randy and Debbie Robison

Paul Selby

Sue and Butch Skiles

Norval and Nedra Smith

Snow Bird Antiques
Karla Johnson
Waukesha, Wisconsin

Warren K. Sparks

Spotswood Antique Shop
J. D., Pauline, and S. L. Sonifrank
Rocky's Antique Mall
Weyer's Cave, Virginia

Evelyn Staples
Antiqueland Mall
Madison, Alabama

Mr. and Mrs. William Thurston

Twickenham Antiques
Antiqueland Mall
Madison, Alabama

The Victorian Connoisseur
Dick and Vickie Ridle
Pekin, Illinois

Village Square Antiques
Glen and Theresa Nance
Pochahontas, Illinois

Appie Watkins
Carriage House Antiques
Columbia Antique Mall
Columbia, South Carolina

Carolyn Watson
Antiqueland Mall
Madison, Alabama

❧ Preface ❧

"I like the organization of your first Victorian book better than the second," a Pennsylvania dealer remarked. "It was easier to find chairs, tables, dressers, and sideboards in it. When you divided the second one into styles and years of popularity, some chairs were under Louis XV, others were in the Renaissance chapter, while another group was segregated as Eastlake."

That dealer's criticism helped. In an endeavor to give readers more facts and to help them learn about the various styles that prevailed throughout the Victorian era, the furniture in *Book II* was categorized by style and approximate dates of manufacture. The dealer helped us see that this format was not handy when people wanted an overall view of dressers, for example, or a quick, approximate value of an article at an auction, show, or shop.

Book I was organized by rooms where a particular piece of furniture might be found. For example, most dressers, cupboards, desks, and chairs were in the same chapter. Now for *Book III,* we're trying a new format. Each type of furniture is grouped in its own chapter. You'll find chapters on seating, tables and stands, cupboards and cabinets, children's possessions, and bedchamber furnishings. Hopefully, these categories will be more convenient for reference. If you find them so, thank Terry in Pennsylvania for his observation.

An Alabama reader called not long ago to tell us he had purchased a parlor set similar to one in our book. He had bought his at an auction for much less than the suggested retail value. Since he was restoring an antebellum home, he was interested in learning about authentic-looking fabrics, colors, and accessories. We have received other calls of this nature. Because of this, Chapter Ten covers accessories, and suggestions about drapes, rugs, colors, and fabrics appear in Chapter Eleven.

Getting to know Victoriana is a continual learning process, best done by visiting museums, historic sites, antiques shops, and shows where furniture is displayed. Ask questions. Read books. Examine articles carefully. There is always more information available for anyone with an inquiring mind.

The pictures in our three books on Victorian furniture styles and prices are different in each volume. While the basic facts presented are the same, there is new material in every book. The following is an overview of the three:

BOOK I: Organized by rooms. Stresses walnut furniture. Contains prices from 1876 with the original names of furniture used when possible. "The Victorian Age" chart classifies the styles as early, mid, and late Victorian, beginning with spool furniture of the 1820s to 1870s and ending with the introduction of mission and golden oak at the era's end. Naturally Louis XV rococo, Renaissance Revival, and Eastlake are included. Questionnaires on prices were sent out to antiques dealers throughout the country, and answers came from Hawaii to Maine, from California to the Carolinas. The book includes a summary of this price study.

BOOK II: Chapters present styles and periods. Contents include the total Victorian era — not just walnut, but also oak, wire, metal, wicker, country, painted, and the Empire of 1840 through the new Empire of the early 1900s. Includes English imports, reproductions and how to recognize them, a cost comparison between furniture that is ready to use and other that needs repair, prices of cut-down tables, main characteristics of nineteenth-century furniture, and an index.

BOOK III: Organized by object — chairs, tables, beds, etc. Covers formal furniture made of walnut, cherry, rosewood, and mahogany, with a few chestnut and oak examples. Also includes chapters on decor and accessories, and a chart with pictures illustrating each substyle and dates of popularity. A chapter on famous names in the furniture industry discusses Belter, Jelliff, Meeks, and others. Includes an index.

At an antiques show book booth, a couple asked to have a Victorian book autographed. It was marked "revised" on the cover, meaning that the publisher issued revised copies when the edition sold out or prices needed updating. For a revision, the authors collect and supply current prices and send in new color photographs for the revised edition. The cover changes, too, but the black-and-white photos and the text remain the same. All updates of this kind display the word "revised" on the cover. Knowing this may save you from buying two copies of the same book.

The contents of *Book I, Book II,* and *Book III* vary in their texts, photographs, and formats, and each presents a different gallery of Victorian pictures. In total, well over one thousand illustrations can be found in this series.

❧ 1 ❧
The Price Is Right

A price book is merely a guidebook. It suggests the cost of objects, but it is not the ultimate authority on their value.

In pricing antiques, supply and demand are important factors. For example, if an article is rare, beautiful, and sought after, those who covet it will be willing to pay well to acquire it. Another item may be scarce, but if it is not as popular, its market value will be lower.

The condition of an object is also of prime importance. In furniture, pristine examples are more valuable than those which require repairs or have been covered with paint, possibly to hide blemishes, burns, gouges, or water or ink stains.

Demand differs by region. For example, a Connecticut dealer may do well selling country styles in her state, but may offer Empire pieces through her shop in New York City.

To gather information for this book, we have traveled thousands of miles taking pictures, making observations, and chatting with collectors and dealers. There are no museum pictures included. All the objects shown are in homes or on display in shops. In this book, each object is labeled with the name of the state in which it was photographed, along with its actual price or a value assigned to it by its owner.

❧ 2 ❧
What's Victorian?

"I will be good," the twelve-year-old girl promised solemnly.

This was not the statement of a contrite child. It was the sincere pledge of Alexandrina Victoria (1819-1901) when, for the first time, she was told that she would one day be crowned queen of the United Kingdom of Great Britain and Ireland. She was eighteen years old when her uncle William IV died on June 20, 1837, and the traditional shouts of the saddened citizens rang out, "The king is dead. Long live the queen."

Queen Victoria endeavored to keep the promise she had made six years before. Her reign of sixty-three years established a new record for British monarchs. During that same period, eighteen presidents (if Grover Cleveland's split terms are counted separately) served the American people. From childhood, Victoria was educated in politics and government so that she understood state matters and was instilled with a feeling for democracy. During her reign, the Island's population more than doubled as British leadership expanded into Asia and Africa and the British Empire reached its pinnacle of power.

Victoria's reign was also a time of transition marked by industrialization, with factory machines replacing hand workmanship. Unprecedented prosperity reached the growing middle class. The newly developed railroads, telephones, and telegraph lines linked the nation. On August 16, 1858, Queen Victoria and President James Buchanan exchanged greetings via the recently completed transcontinental cable, which was laid under the Atlantic Ocean. Roads spanned the nation, and literature flourished. As the year 1879 ended, the news of Thomas A. Edison's invention of the electric incandescent light amazed the world, and when Benjamin Harrison was president (1889-1893), he had a choice between the use of gas or electric illumination in the White House. A strange "horseless carriage" was cranked into motion after the first successful gasoline-powered automobile in the United States was driven at Springfield, Massachusetts, in 1893.

Revolution of a peaceful, scientific, and industrial nature seemed to prevail everywhere.

Queen Victoria's marriage to her cousin, Prince Albert of Germany, was a happy union, producing nine royal children. Because Prince Consort Albert was interested in the welfare of the people, the queen sought his advice and business acumen when she made many important governmental decisions. After Albert died from typhoid fever in 1861, Victoria retired from social life. For forty years she sentimentally kept their royal rooms just as they had been when Albert lived. His writing materials remained on the desk, and his garments were kept as if they were to be worn soon. Despite this tendency to relive the past, Victoria continued to perform her state duties, as she guided her country to its leadership role among the nations of the world.

Perhaps it was partly because of her loyalty to the British Empire that more than half of the nineteenth century is named for her — the Victorian era. And furniture crafted during this time span, 1837 to 1901, is referred to as Victorian in style.

Sixty-three years? That's a long time for one person to be a world leader. And it is too long for fashions to remain unchanged. At the beginning of Victoria's reign, crinoline, a stiff cloth made of horsehair and linen, was a must for the elegant, well-dressed woman. Her hoop skirt swayed and gave her a bell shape. In the 1870s, the hoop was passé. Instead, fullness popped up behind and was padded with a bustle to give a modish lady a bulging derrière. By the 1900s, the long skirts were form fitting, slim, and trim.

In furniture, too, styles changed. But because those changes were gradual and styles overlapped, it is necessary to assign approximate years to the periods when they were in vogue. In the past, what was considered passé in an urban setting might have retained its popularity much longer in rural locales. Frequently when changes did come about, the furniture makers produced what has been termed transitional styles, which combined some qualities of the current look with those

Walnut hall tree with fretwork, metal umbrella drip pans, and white marble top; 34″ wide, 13″ deep, 89″ high. In Illinois, **$850.**

Mahogany Empire sewing stand with crotch mahogany veneer on drawer fronts; paw feet, sandwich pulls; 23″ wide, 19″ deep, 32″ high. In Illinois, **$900.**

of the new trend. Therefore, it is necessary to examine American Empire furniture (circa 1815-1840s) because it was the predecessor of early Victorian styles. It, too, is related to royalty.

The powerful Napoleon Bonaparte of France inspired Empire furniture. Of royal Italian lineage, Napoleon was not an heir to the French throne, but seized the crown for his own. Many historians rate Napoleon as one of the greatest military strategists of all times, as well as an an able administrator. They record that his troops affectionately dubbed him the Little Corporal and loyally followed wherever he led.

At various times, Napoleon wanted to conquer Egypt and all of Europe, including England. The cadence of his marching armies beat fear into the hearts of many nations. Even across the Atlantic Ocean, the United States

felt the pulsations. President Thomas Jefferson (1801-1809) thought the Little Corporal might covet North America. Fortunately, Napoleon needed finances more than land so he negotiated a business deal with the United States. France had claimed a vast territory that encompassed approximately one million square miles, bordering on the western edge of the infant nation. In 1803, the United States purchased this property for about fifteen million dollars in order to rid themselves of this pugnacious, greedy neighbor.

Napoleon was in and out of power from 1799 to 1815. While he ruled, his vanity was bigger than he was, and he had furniture designed especially for him. The royal Bonaparte "Bee" was embroidered in gold on upholstery fabric, and white silk was considered luxurious. But generally, hardy rather than soft materials were selected, especially in the primary colors of red, yellow, and blue. Dark greens and browns also were popular. A carved crown, an N for Napoleon, or a replica of the royal head might be incorporated into the designs on chairs, settees, or case pieces. Since France's armies had battled in Egypt, designers incorporated the sphinx into their works and borrowed generously from Greek and Roman styles. Mythology provided figures used in showy, ornate, excessively ornamented, heavy, rectangular furniture. A rich appearance was achieved through exotic woods, mahogany, rosewood, and ebony. Gilt or brass mounts, referred to as *ormolu*, were in the form of wings, wreaths, or swags. Acanthus leaves and laurel branches provided attractive designs. Cornucopias, swords, shields, and torches were prevalent.

Just as French is translated into English, the Empire style was interpreted on this side of the Atlantic. Furniture makers were free to take or leave what they liked or disliked in Empire. The style influenced American furniture from about 1815 through the 1840s. It waned earlier in Europe because Napoleon was exiled in 1815 following his defeat by the British armies, and his furniture exited with him.

The early American Empire is closer to the French form than the later versions. Naturally, chic women requested Empire designs from their cabinetmakers. Even the noted craftsman Duncan Phyfe, who moved his shop from Albany to New York City in about 1790, had to switch from his dainty, graceful creations to the hearty new styles to please his name-dropping clientele. His earlier work was usually in mahogany, but after 1830 he turned to rosewood. Most critics believe that delicacy of line was his forte and that his artistry and quality both declined with the demand for hefty styles.

The factory system, with its steam-operated band saw, helped laborers take over the furniture-making industry. When row upon row of bedsteads, tables, chests, and chairs were produced rapidly by machine, the gradual demise of the cabinetmaker and his personal relationship to his customers was inevitable. No longer would thick pieces of mahogany be hand carved to please a client's tastes.

The New York City cabinetmakers Joseph Meeks and Sons may have been first to replace excessive leaf and plume carvings with the simpler curves of the pillar and scroll. But John Hall popularized this switch. His book, *The Cabinet Maker's Assistant,* published in Baltimore in 1840, illustrated his ideas. The newly invented band saw, activated by steam power, could create massive scrolls with ease. When a layer of mahogany or rosewood veneer was glued over an inexpensive wood, the result had an elegant look that appealed to middle-class, style-conscious buyers who wanted to copy the home decor of affluent society matrons but financially were unable to do so.

Pillars stood stoically, matched to perfection, on the stiles of chests of drawers and desks. Thick table tops were supported by massive pillars, which terminated in platforms with scrolled feet. Daintiness was taboo, as this hearty, heavy furniture prevailed throughout the 1840s. Because of its intrusion into the Victorian time period, some authorities include it under that category, but its hippopotamus size qualifies it for a Late Empire classification. The following chart covering the years of Queen Victoria's reign includes this formal furniture.

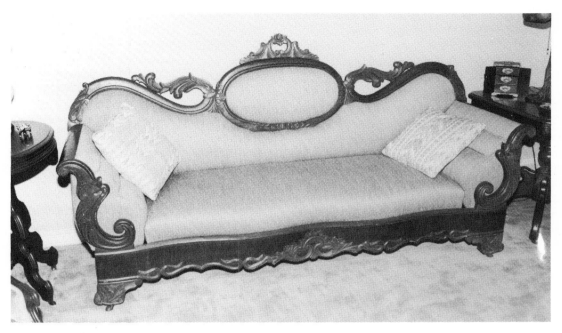

Walnut and mahogany Empire transitional sofa with medallion back, 84″ arm to arm, 42″ high. In Texas, **$1,700.**

Mahogany Empire game table with acanthus leaves on pedestal and paw feet, 35″ wide, 17″ deep, 28″ high. In Illinois, **$725.**

Style	Dates	Characteristics	Wood
American Empire	1815-1840s	Early pieces were handmade. Heavy lines. Both marble and wooden tops. Symmetrical. Rectangular shapes. Ogee frames. Beading. Wings as feet on sofas. Paw feet. Acanthus leaf and laurel branch swags. Cornucopias. Elaborate hand carving of thick wood. Cabinetmakers often used chisels. Round wooden drawer pulls or metal lion's-head back plates with rings. Inspired by Napoleon.	Mahogany, rosewood, some ebony. 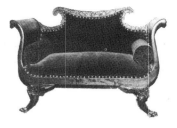

Late American Empire	1840-1850	Massive, heavy. Mainly factory produced with new steam-powered circular and band saws that replaced hand carving. Massive C- and S-shaped scrolls. Pillars on stiles of case pieces. John Hall's book, *The Cabinet Makers' Assistant,* published in 1840, helped popularize this style.	Veneer used extensively. Mahogany, later rosewood. 

Early Victorian

Hitchcock's Fancy Chairs	1820-1850	Mass produced. Stenciled designs in bright paint. Signed on back edge of seat with some form of Hitchcock name. Knocked down when shipped to national market. Other companies made fancy chairs also, but Hitchcock is the generic name.	Soft woods, combination of woods. 
Spool Furniture	1820-1870	Machined, resembling a string of spools, knobs, or buttons. Usually stained mahogany. Almost country in style. Straight turnings were easier than curved ones before the lathe was used, so curved bedstead headboards are later, probably dating to the mid-1800s. Sometimes called Jenny Lind.	Mostly maple at first. Some cherry and walnut. Soft woods used later. 

Gothic Revival	1820-1850, again in the 1870s	Light in appearance. Tracery, points, arches like church window. Made in limited supply. Patterned after Gothic architecture. Clocks shaped to peak at the top to resemble an old-fashioned church spire were called steeple clocks. Chair backs peaked. Cathedral-like carvings or ornamentations on some case pieces.	Walnut 

Mid Victorian

Louis XV Revival	1840-1865	French style that imitated Louis XV (reigned 1715-1774). Rococo (rock shell, flora, fauna) carvings. Elliptical shapes used more than round. Curves, not straight lines. Marble tops common. Rich upholstery fabrics, but horsehair predominated. Spiral springs. Cabriole legs. Fancy fruit, nut, and leaf carved handles. Finger-roll furniture frames. Pierced carving.	Walnut, some rosewood and mahogany. 

Cottage Furniture	1845-1890	Country type, inexpensive. Simple lines. Painted and stenciled with fruits, sheaves of wheat, pastoral scenes, flowers. Often artificially grained to resemble a more expensive wood. Sometimes had walnut applied decorations and handles.	Pine 

Renaissance Revival	1850-1885	Tall. High bedsteads, secretary desks, sideboards. Machine made, frequently with hand-carved details. Elaborate. Carved crests and pediments. Roundels. Huge dressing case mirrors. Carved wooden pulls. Ebony and gilt handles (teardrops). Pedestals with cluttered bases. Turned finials. Urns. Columbia (carved head of a woman symbolizing the U.S.) circa 1876. Many marble tops.	Walnut

Late Victorian

Patented Combination Furniture	Late 1800s	Many varieties. Highchair that converted to stroller, bed that folded into a desk, platform rockers.	Walnut, maple, oak, light woods.

Eastlake	1870-1890	Rebellion against fancy furniture. England's Eastlake tried to bring distinctive design into furniture, but simplicity was overwhelmed by machine details and became cluttered. Rectangular, straight lines. Incised lines. Chip carving.	Walnut

Golden Oak	1890-1920	Yellowish color. Pressed brass bail handles. Pressed design on chair backs. Round pedestal extension dining room tables. China cabinets with convex glass. Paw feet. Rectangular dining tables with bulbous legs. Combination furniture, such as beds that fold into chests or desks, fall-front desks with bookcase sides. Reproductions being made today.	Oak

The chart mentions the major furniture styles of the period. But there was also lacy iron furniture that graced lawns and sun rooms and even invaded the bedchamber from about 1850 through 1900. Brass beds or iron ones with brass trim or plating were a change from the robust wooden Renaissance and Eastlake frames. Wicker (the generic term for fibers such as rush, willow, and reed) was prevalent from about the mid-1840s through the end of the Victorian era. The religious Shakers contributed clean-lined, functional, country furniture. And the end of Victoria's reign saw the introduction of Mission oak, with its stark, straight, square lines; and bird's-eye maple, with markings that resembled eyes.

There were Oriental influences, Turkish styles, and Jacobean revivals. Victorians took what they liked from all the former periods, combined them, gave the mongrel furniture a fancy name, and sold it to those who sought the latest styles. This eclecticism (selecting from various sources) was possible because of steam-operated machines in factories that mass produced furniture.

Remember that some furniture does not have distinguishing characteristics and could be around for countless years. For example, thousands of cane-bottom side chairs with slat backs are look-alikes, and the common washstand was a design standard for a long time. The term "circa" (about) is handy when it is not possible to date a piece exactly.

This book's main emphasis is walnut, but elite rosewood, the choice of many connoisseurs, is included too. Almost as if they were cloned, some walnut styles were executed in less expensive and less favored woods of the time period. For example, a pioneering furniture catalog was developed by Nelson Matter & Company, Manufacturers of Furniture, Grand Rapids, Michigan, in 1873, at a time when photography was still in its infancy. In their 1876 catalog, three-piece ash bedroom sets, including bureau, washstand, and bedstead, were listed for $23.75 to $46.75. They were stained to resemble walnut, the queen of the line. Similarly designed "chamber suits" in walnut sold for $27.50 to $51. Simultaneously, ash's look-alike, chestnut, was sold for even less and went through an inferiority stage as a stand-in for walnut.

Walnut common washstand with turned towel bar ends, 24" wide, 16" deep, 33" high. In Iowa, **$215.**

17

❧ 3 ❧
Welcome to Our Home

"Come in. Come right on in!"

That's the cheery invitation that should be conveyed by an entrance hall, the area that makes a home's first impression. The hall should be attractive, with intriguing items that make guests want to explore the home's decor.

A well-known interior designer states that color is noticed first. If you can't splurge on wallpapers, brighten up with paint. The designer likes to frame figured cloth to accentuate, bring out the hues, and create a dramatic effect. He feels that the comfort of visitors should be paramount and suggests that even a mini-sized entrance can have a mirror so guests can smooth windblown hair on arrival or arrange a hat or scarf on departure. A small shelf is helpful for cumbersome articles, and a little chair or stool makes it easier to remove or put on boots. To this designer, these items in a hall extend a warm welcome.

For Victorians, hall stands almost served as silent butlers. They included stationary or adjustable brass or iron hooks or wooden knobs to hold hats or coats. Circular arms held umbrellas erect as they dripped dry into decorative metal pans inserted at the base. Customarily, these receptacles were cast from pot metal or brass, and the pans could be removed for cleaning. Some were shell shaped, but others were plain, functional squares or circles. Today the stands are generally referred to as hall trees.

Pier mirrors, like wallflowers, remained aloof and out-of-touch, since they occupied the space between two tall windows or some other narrow area. Large models standing almost to the ceiling sometimes incorporated a shelf or drawer, possibly with marble. Smaller, vertical versions hung over a table that was placed against a wall. When Gothic furniture, with its tracery, arches, and points, was in fashion, chairs with a cathedral appearance were featured in halls. They had a formal, dignified air as they sat lined up ready to receive callers. The Gothic revival styles were present from about 1820-1850 and were resurrected in the 1870s. Some Gothic was mixed with rococo, and a mongrel breed resulted. Gothic lines prevailed in library furniture and bedrooms also, but the parlors and living rooms of the mid-Victorian years were mainly furnished with rococo. The Gothic styles represented an English influence on furniture.

Victorian families could congregate in the sitting room, but the parlor was out of bounds. It was reserved for special occasions and for special people. When the minister came to call, the parlor's doors would be opened. Seldom-seen relatives or a daughter's beau could be entertained there. Its furniture was the best that a home had to offer. Children had to sit stiff and straight in the stuffy parlor, usually on slippery horsehair upholstery. Small children whose feet didn't reach the floor had to brace themselves to keep from sliding off. Since homes ordinarily served the family from the womb to the tomb, a loved one's coffin might be placed on a low table supplied by the undertaker. The memorial service could be conducted at home or at the church according to the desires of the family. In the homes of the common people, the parlor was indeed reserved and was always orderly since it was so seldom occupied.

When people stereotype Victorian era furnishings, they are apt to conjure up pictures of a lady's and gentleman's chair set. These pairs were introduced during the 1840s and kept steady company for more than thirty years. Graceful dignity characterized the rococo examples, with their rounded, usually tufted backs. Flowers often were carved on the aprons and on the knees of the cabriole legs. A floral crest on the frame of the back was common. The man's chair had padded arms and more generous proportions, while the lady's version was more dainty and had braces or demi-arms.

The style of the lady's chair may not seem as comfortable as the man's, but it accommodated the full skirts of the time. A seamstress might use more than thirty-five yards of fabric for one fashionable dress. It would be difficult to confine all that bulk within the limits of an armchair.

Walnut hall tree with small lift-top wooden box, shell-and-flower design drip pan; 31″ wide, 13″ deep, 89″ high. In Illinois, **$1,145.**

Walnut Eastlake pier mirror with rope pilasters, incised lines, and pink marble shelf, 26″ wide, 11″ deep, 87″ high. In Pennsylvania, **$395.**

Hoop skirts were in vogue during this time, and horrors, how could a lady sit down without exposing an ankle or a limb? (The word "leg" was too vulgar, so "limb" was substituted.) Victorians were a prudish breed. If a lady sat down without care, her hoop could flare up and expose embarrassing underpinnings. To prevent this, a lady learned to squeeze together the rearward rings of her skirt as she backed into a chair. Therefore, it was a practical consideration, not discrimination, that determined where a man or a woman would sit.

Side chairs frequently had "balloon" backs, so called because their shape roughly resembled a hot-air balloon soaring in the sky. Their round seats were upholstered in horsehair (a somber black cloth formed by weaving linen threads together with hair from the manes and tails of horses), needlework, velvet, damask, satin, plush, and brocatelle fabrics. When the wooden frame of a chair or sofa was decorated with a continuous concave molding, it was referred to as a finger-roll frame. Scrolls, shells, fruits, nuts, and flowers added ornamental touches.

Victorian rococo furniture, with its themes inspired by nature, could be ornate and exotic, especially when pierced carving techniques created leaf- and grape-filled vines surrounding a leaf-shaped upholstered back on a side chair. Add spiral or twisted legs and stiles with an Elizabethan, Jacobean, or Flemish flair, and the result was an eclectic example of the Victorian furniture maker's workmanship.

The Renaissance Revival (roughly 1850-1885) brought with it squared lines, a definite change from the continuous curves of rococo. Features were still borrowed from earlier styles. There continued to be a great deal of carving, but much of it had a geometric background rather than a Mother Nature feel. The roses and grapes were generally replaced by roundels. In the Midwest, applied panels or strips of burl veneer often were accompanied

Walnut Louis XV substyle matching lady's and gentleman's chairs with oval backs, finger roll, open arms, and button tufting. In Iowa, **$850** the set.

by incised lines, sometimes accentuated with gilt for a decorative touch. New York furniture makers liked the effect they achieved through the use of inlaid ornamentations. The gentle curves of the rococo cabriole leg were replaced by stouter turned versions. Crests on chairs had a geometric look. Porcelain, brass, mother-of-pearl, terra-cotta, or carved wooden medallions might be included. Frequently a human head was the model for small plaques of this type. As a rule, Renaissance Revival furniture had a stouter appearance than its more feminine rococo counterpart.

English architect Charles Lock(e) Eastlake (1836-1906) became concerned about the contents of the homes he designed and built. Eastlake felt furniture should be functional, yet stylish. To help do away with his peers' tendency toward eclecticism and to develop careful design in furnishings, he wrote a book with the impressive title *Hints on Household Taste, Furnishings, Upholstery and Other Details*, published around 1868. There was no doubt in his mind that curves wasted wood, lacked comfort, and did not have the strength that straight lines offered. What could be better and more aesthetically pleasing than a straight, boxlike construction, especially when it was made out of sturdy oak?

It took some time before this latest fashion from the British Isles crossed the Atlantic. But eventually, American manufacturers latched onto Eastlake's ideas and a new trend developed. The Eastlake style grew and matured in America from 1870 to 1890.

United States designers introduced a few innovations — including some that Eastlake might have found objectionable. Although the

Walnut Louis XV substyle balloon-back side chair with molded cresting, 37″ high. In Iowa, **$150.**

Walnut Louis XV substyle side chair with splat back and cabriole legs, 36″ high. In Pennsylvania, **$195.**

vast American walnut forests were diminishing rapidly, dark walnut was selected for Eastlake furniture. Appendages and clutter were added to the rectangles and squares. Chip carving and parallel incised lines were featured frequently. These parallel lines have been named "railroad tracks" for obvious reasons.

Eastlake's rebellion sired a new trend in furniture design, and his name is still associated with boxy styles. The use of dark walnut declined, partly because the wood was becoming scarce, but also because golden oak caught fashion's fancy at the end of the nineteenth century. Some housewives turned to brass and iron furnishings (circa 1850-1900) in order to acquire a new look. While Eastlake's influence would be remembered, his ideas became passé.

Rosewood side chair with carved grapes and leaves in pierced back, twisted legs and back supporting columns; 46″ high. In Texas, **$950.**

Close-up of back of rosewood side chair.

Another style produced by the tens of thousands in the nineteenth century was the cane-bottom chair. Its frame, including the legs, front rung, and the back splat (vertical support) or crosswise slats give clues as to the age of the chair. For example, a flat rung or one that is slightly concave was popular at a time when women's skirts were exceedingly full. Today, some people like to call these rungs "hoop-skirt rungs." Hand-woven seats and backs made from cane (strips from the stems of the rattan, a climbing palm tree) were not a Victorian innovation. Examples exist from colonial American times.

Folding chairs, both straight and rocking, could be called fireside chairs as well. Just as moderns tuck away their card-table chairs, Victorians stored these folding chairs and brought them out when extra seating was required. They also could be moved easily to

the hearth for warmth. Some examples retain their carpet upholstery fabric, but most have had a facelift and are covered in velvet.

While rockers are considered comforting in the United States, Europeans sometimes fear that they will tip and toss their occupants to the floor. Rocking chairs made their debut in the late 1700s, and visitors to this continent thought they were both ridiculous and dangerous. Wouldn't those detractors be astonished to know that rocking chairs have continued to please people for more than two hundred years?

Occasionally, the therapeutic benefits of rockers are noted by the medical profession. For example, when a physician recommended that President John F. Kennedy use a rocker to ease his backaches, the chairs almost became a status symbol. Despite this, one woman of Swiss origin likes to know that her rocker will stay in one place. She selects one that sways on a platform. She feels that this type doesn't wear out rugs as chairs with narrow rockers (sometimes called carpet cutters) do.

Sofas, love seats, and settees are elongated chairs. Love seats (or courting chairs) are made for two, while a settee is twice or more the width of a chair. It may have an upholstered seat, with or without exposed wood on the back. A sofa, designed for multiple occupants, has both an upholstered seat and back.

The French originated coil springs for upholstered furniture in the 1700s, and gradually their idea spread. It is thought that sofas were not made in the United States until introduced in Philadelphia in the mid-1820s. As with the chairs, frames varied and reflected the time period in which they were created. By today's

terminology, a cameo, medallion, or mirror back designates an oval or rounded wooden loop that frames some of the upholstery fabric in the sofa's back. Frequently, buttons were sewn through the upholstery material to hold it in place. The arrangement of the buttons and the resulting folds in the material formed patterns that are termed tufting or button tufting. When the design of the frame looks like it is slithering, it is referred to as serpentine in shape. High points on the back are called crestings, and some have pegs on them so that these wooden crest rails can be inserted or removed at will.

One special sofa was designed with a low section in the middle of the back and tall back supports at each side. Behind the sofa sat a small table. Another out-of-the-ordinary sofa

Walnut Renaissance Revival armchair with burl veneer raised panels, applied roundels, and girl's profile in medallion below molded crest; 32″ arm to arm, 42″ high. In Texas, **$375.**

Walnut Eastlake side chair with incised lines and demi arms, 37″ high. In Pennsylvania, **$225.**

Walnut cane-seat chair with hand hold in top slat and flat or hoop-skirt front rung, 33″ high. In Indiana, **$95.**

Walnut Eastlake armchair with incised lines, 26″ arm to arm, 42″ high. In Illinois, **$295.**

frame is pierce-carved in the design of bunches of grapes and a hungry bird. A medallion back at one end invites a person to sit, and the other end is united to the chair-like portion by a sweeping rococo S curve. It's amazing that piercing a solid piece of walnut could create distinctive designs that give a rich appearance to sofas.

Normally, a "parlor suite" consisted of from three to seven pieces that matched in contour, carvings, leg style, turnings, and upholstery fabric. There could be a sofa or a love seat, four side chairs, an armchair, and one with partial arms. A small set offered a love seat with two chairs. Of course, there were more extensive suites available for more pretentious homes. Today's interior designers do not promote such families of furniture. Sample pieces from an

eleven-piece rococo suite are shown in this chapter. The set is made up of a sofa, eight side chairs, and two armchairs. See Chapter Nine to examine pictures of suites that have been attributed to well-known American furniture makers of the nineteenth century.

There were other upholstered seats also. A chaise longue was designed for reclining. This couchlike chair provided a back support for the sitter and an extended area that accommodated a person's legs. Many styles were available down through the years. Today they frequently are referred to as fainting couches.

A tête-à-tête is a petite sofa or love seat, in which the two seats face in opposite directions so that the couple can see each other. It is united by an S-shaped, continuous curve. This was a Victorian innovation of the mid-1800s

Walnut Eastlake fireside folding carpet rocker with incised lines. In Alabama, **$240.**

Walnut rocking chair with cane seat and back, scrolled arms; 21″ arm to arm, 40″ high. In Ohio, **$155.**

that took advantage of the laminating and bending techniques perfected by the famous German cabinetmaker, John Belter. His successful steam molding of layers of wood made such sinuous shapes possible. He and other creative craftsmen helped make Victorian furniture distinctive.

Walnut Louis XV substyle love seat with button-tufted back, 46″ wide, 35″ high. In Iowa, **$750.**

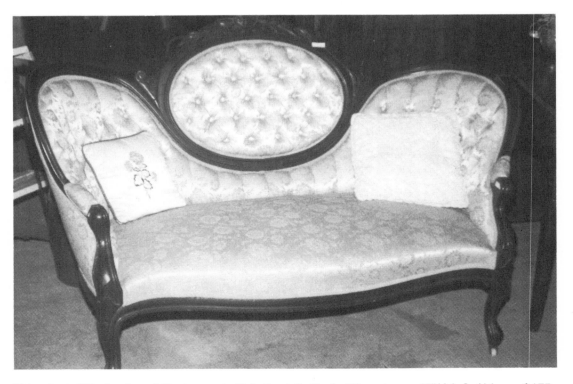

Walnut Louis XV substyle medallion love seat with button-tufted back, 47″ arm to arm, 37″ high. In Alabama, **$475.**

Rosewood and cherry upholstered side chair, armchair, and sofa from an eleven-piece set including one sofa, two armchairs, and eight side chairs with nut and rose carving on crests. In Texas, **$7,500** for the eleven-piece set.

Walnut hall tree with pierced back, oval mirror, and marble top over drawer; 15″ wide, 11″ deep, 70″ high. In Pennsylvania, **$475.**

Walnut hall tree with pierced back, applied decorations, molded pediment, marble top over drawer, and two metal drip pans; 34″ wide, 12″ deep, 90″ high. In Pennsylvania, **$675.**

Walnut Renaissance Revival hall tree with molded and paneled pediment, marble top over drawer, and two metal drip pans; 36″ wide, 14″ deep, 95″ high. In Texas, **$1,495.**

Walnut hall tree with pierced back, two shell-design metal drip pans, and a wooden top over the drawer; 28″ wide, 16″ deep, 84″ high. In Pennsylvania, **$525.**

Walnut Renaissance Revival hall tree with molded, arched pediment, burl veneer raised panels, marble top over drawer, and two shell-design metal drip pans; 41″ wide, 12″ deep, 90″ high. In Arkansas, **$1,000.**

Walnut Eastlake pier mirror with applied decorations, molded and incised pediment, and marble shelf; 24″ wide, 8″ deep, 95″ high. In Missouri, **$550.**

Walnut Renaissance Revival hall tree with molded and paneled pediment, burl veneer raised panels, marble over drawer, porcelain tips on coat hooks, and two metal drip pans; 46″ wide, 14″ deep, 89″ high. In Iowa, **$1,595.**

Walnut Eastlake pier mirror with molded pediment, incised lines, pilasters, and white marble shelf; 25″ wide, 12″ deep, 100″ high. In Iowa, **$495.**

Walnut Eastlake pier mirror with molded and incised pediment, burl veneer raised panels, and white marble shelf; 25″ wide, 12″ deep, 94″ high. In Iowa, **$520.**

Walnut rococo and Gothic side chair with molded front apron, cabriole legs, and scrolling stiles, circa 1850; 35″ high. In Pennsylvania, **$150.**

Walnut Eastlake armchair with incised lines, 29″ arm to arm, 32″ high. In Maryland, **$395.**

Oak Gothic-style hall chair with original leather and incised lines. Made by "Wm. Drufrock, fine upholstered furniture, St. Louis;" 21″ wide, 57″ high. In Virginia, **$300.**

Close-up of crest design on Gothic-style hall chair.

Walnut slipper-type chair, 33″ wide, 29″ high. In Illinois, **$325.**

Walnut Renaissance Revival, Eastlake-influence matching lady's and gentleman's chairs with incised lines, burl veneer raised panels, and carved head of Minerva (Greek goddess of wisdom and war) on crest. In Indiana, **$750** the set.

Walnut Renaissance Revival, Eastlake influence side chair with incised lines, applied burl panels, and a molded crest; 38″ high. In Illinois, **$165.**

Walnut Louis XV substyle matching lady's and gentleman's chairs with oval backs, finger roll, open arms, carved grape and leaf cresting, and button tufting. In Iowa, **$850** the set.

Walnut side chair showing Eastlake influence, with incised lines and burl veneer panels; 40″ high. In Iowa, **$250.**

Walnut rococo and Gothic side chair with applied carving on apron and knees of legs, 36″ high. In Illinois, **$295.**

Rosewood side chair with carved crest, interlocking C's and scrolls, and button-tufted back; 24″ arm to arm, 40″ high. One of a pair. In Texas, **$2,500** the set.

Rosewood chaise longue, sometimes called "fainting couch;" 69″ wide, 30″ high. In Texas, **$1,500.**

Walnut Louis XV substyle modified spoon-back gentleman's chair, 25″ arm to arm, 42″ high. In Pennsylvania, **$450.**

Walnut Louis XV substyle side chair with finger roll and cabriole legs, 20″ arm to arm, 35″ high. In Pennsylvania, **$250.**

Walnut sofa. The back-rail crest and arms, extending to the feet, are carved from one piece of solid walnut, but the decoration on the apron is applied. 74″ wide, 39″ high. In Arkansas, **$2,500.**

Walnut Renaissance Revival, Eastlake influence side chair with incised lines and molded-paneled crest; 35″ high. In Iowa **$250.**

Walnut Renaissance Revival, Eastlake influence side chair with incised lines, burl veneer raised panels, applied pierced-molded crest, and heart-shaped, button-tufted back; 38″ high. In Texas, **$300.**

Walnut chaise longue with applied roundels and a molded crest, 75″ wide, 34″ high. In Pennsylvania, **$400.**

Rosewood sewing chair with carved and molded cresting, turned supporting columns; 41″ high. In Missouri, **$400.**

Walnut armchair with needlepoint seat (originally caned), 23″ arm to arm, 38″ high. In Pennsylvania, **$175.**

Rosewood sofa with pierced, carved crest, 77″ arm to arm, 48″ high. In Missouri, **$800.**

Walnut barbershop chair with velvet upholstery and swan heads on arms, 28″ arm to arm, 45″ high. In Illinois, **$1,200** with footrest step-stool.

Footrest step-stool that accompanies barbershop chair, 27″ high.

Walnut Eastlake armchair with incised lines, 27″ arm to arm, 31″ high. In Alabama, **$175.**

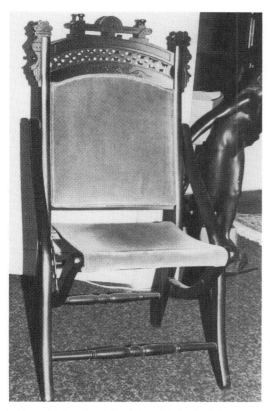

Walnut folding fireside chair with incised lines and pierced back, 36″ high. In Maryland, **$125.**

Walnut side chair with needlepoint seat, burl veneer raised panels, and splat back; 37″ high. The original seat was caned. In Indiana, **$150.**

Walnut cane-seat chair with incised lines and spindles, 36″ high. One of a set of five. In Alabama, **$750** the set.

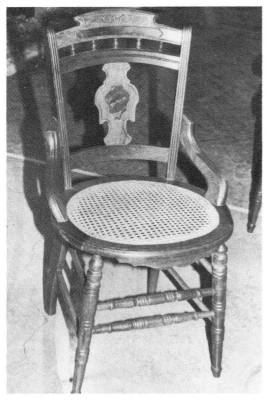

Walnut cane-seat chair with splat back and incised lines, 34″ high. One of a set of six. In Illinois, **$175** each.

Walnut cane-seat chair with veneer trim, incised lines, splat back, and demi arms; 34″ high. In Indiana, **$95.**

Walnut matching armchair and demi armchair with incised lines and framed backs enclosing a center splat. In Iowa, **$175** each.

Walnut chair with cane seat and back, burl veneer raised panels on front rung, front legs, demi arms, support columns, and crest; 34″ high. In Texas, **$250**.

Walnut cane-seat chair with splat back, veneer trim, and incised lines; 36″ high. One of a set of five. In Illinois, **$250** each.

Maple rocking chair with cane seat and back, 34″ high. In Ohio, **$165**.

Walnut Eastlake rocking chair with cane seat and back. In Texas, **$175**.

Maple Eastlake platform rocker with woven seat and back, burl decoration on crest; 24″ arm to arm, 40″ high. In Pennsylvania, **$250.**

Walnut upholstered platform rocker with carved head of Minerva, the goddess of wisdom and war, at the crest; 24″ wide, 42″ high. In Iowa, **$550.**

Walnut upholstered rocking chair with closed arms, 27″ arm to arm, 36″ high. In Iowa, **$400.**

Walnut upholstered rocking chair, sometimes called Lincoln rocker, with button-tufted back; 24″ arm to arm, 39″ high. In Pennsylvania, **$275.**

Oak upholstered rocking chair with open arms, molded grape and acorn crest; 43″ high. In Iowa, **$300.**

Walnut upholstered platform rocker with incised lines, 24″ arm to arm, 38″ high. In Illinois, **$350.**

Walnut fireside folding rockers, 35″ high. In Iowa, left rocker, **$110;** right rocker, **$125.**

Walnut tête-à-tête with fan backs and pierced carving, 51″ wide, 33″ high. In Texas, **$1,400.**

Walnut upholstered platform rocker with incised lines, patented October 26, 1869; 23″ wide, 42″ high. In Iowa, **$500.**

Walnut Renaissance Revival, Eastlake influence sofa with incised lines, burl veneer raised panels; 63″ arm to arm, 42″ high. In Pennsylvania, **$750.**

Walnut Renaissance Revival, Eastlake influence love seat with incised lines, molded designs; 59″ wide, 43″ high. In Ohio, **$825.**

Walnut Eastlake settee with incised lines, 37″ wide, 21″ deep. In Iowa, **$425.**

Walnut Louis XV substyle oval love seat with button-tufted back, 48″ arm to arm, 37″ high. In Illinois, **$485.**

Rosewood double-medallion love seat with button-tufted back, 56″ wide, 43″ high. In Texas, **$1,500.**

Walnut chair-sofa with pierced carving; 63″ wide, 39″ high at left; 37″ high at right. In Texas, **$1,200.**

Close-up of pierced carving on chair-sofa.

Rosewood double medallion-back with porcelain insert on crest, pierced carving; 69″ wide, 36″ high. In Texas, **$1,250.**

Close-up of porcelain insert on crest of rosewood sofa.

Walnut double round-back sofa with burl paneled divider, swag and tassel apex; 68″ arm to arm, 36″ high. In Texas, **$699.**

Turning the tables was actually a possibility in the Victorian era. Since statues, ornamental glass, and knickknacks were coveted additions to homes, the owners liked to show off their special treasures. If a statue was difficult to lift and examine, it was placed on a table with a revolving top. It was then possible for visitors to admire the item without touching it.

Many small tables held lamps, but plants needed a place to be displayed also. Plant tables came in various sizes. Tops were either round and scalloped to form turtle or clover contours, or rectangular. Some were painted with fancy designs, while others, particularly by New York City furniture makers, were inlaid. These craftsmen often decorated a piece of walnut with tiny inset pieces of wood of various hues to create an attractive pattern. At times, shells, metals, or other materials were used for this delicate, artistic work. Each applied piece had

to be of the same depth in order to create a smooth surface. One table pictured is basically walnut, but includes seven woods, such as teak, rosewood, and birch. Gilt lines and hoof feet create a novel example of Victoriana with a Renaissance feel.

Marble tops were not unique to the time period, but Victorians liked them. Finials (turned, carved, or cast end ornaments) hung down as pendants or thrust upward. It was not unusual to apply a dark stain to hardwood to give it an ebony look. Often, touches of gilt were added. Promoters of the Renaissance and Eastlake styles approved of this dark appearance.

Onyx, with its streaks of rusty gold and color throughout, is a decorative stone often found on small stands. It sometimes was used for the top of a decorative cast brass frame with leaf designs, an onyx and brass finial, and

Walnut lamp table with revolving top and tripod base, 17″ diameter, 27″ high. In Pennsylvania, **$110.**

Walnut Renaissance Revival octagonal-top parlor table with inlaid top; walnut, teak, and rosewood applied decorations; applied roundels; and hooflike feet. In Illinois, **$245.**

paw feet. Plainer, less exotic copies were available through the 1897 Sears Roebuck catalog, in which the highest priced example was recommended as a "handsome wedding present." The genuine gold-plated brass design was "exceedingly bold." A more expensive version, not from the Sears catalog, is pictured in this chapter.

Night stands frequently stood by beds to hold miscellaneous items. A leg formed from a squared block and cut straight did not require as much work as one that was turned. Because this style was used commonly in the mid-1800s in such eastern states as Ohio, Pennsylvania, and New York, some refer to it as a New York leg. A night stand shown with this type of leg is of cherry and has drop leaves. The molding on the two drawers is crimped and may be described as pie crust since it looks as if it were shaped by a homemaker. Small drop-leaf tables with one or two drawers served various purposes, and some are called work tables or sewing tables.

The latter provided compartments where items such as wooden spools, scissors, needles, and pins were stored. A rounded appendage of wood or cloth at the base held mending or fabrics. Frequently, the tables had a hinged top that could be raised. The designs incorporated filigree work, scalloped tops, veneer, and many curves. A rosewood version has a lift lid that, when open, exposes various compartments with inlaid-pattern covers that contrast with the dark wood. There is even a built-in pincushion. The octagonal shape further enhances the piece. Two photographs, showing opened and closed views of the stand, are included in this section.

Another small table with an oval top has a base shelf that was convenient for a tray, creamer, sugar, and teapot. Hence, it was referred to as a teapoy. All the tables could be classified under various titles depending on what the manufacturer called them or the service they performed in a home. Parlor, lamp, work, bedside, or sewing stands were commonly a part of the home in the nineteenth century.

Walnut lamp table with white marble top and tripod base, 16″ diameter, 29″ high. In Pennsylvania, **$250.**

Walnut Renaissance Revival lamp stand with incised lines, ebonized and gilt decoration, 13″ wide, 13″ deep, 38″ high. In Texas, **$500.**

Brass and onyx lamp table with embossed angels on rim, paw feet; 16″ wide, 16″ deep, 31″ high. In Texas, **$350.** Hobbs and Brokunier cranberry opalescent hobnail bowl with applied rim, 8″ diameter, 3½″ high, **$135.**

Cherry drop-leaf work table with pie crust beading on drawers; 22″ wide, 19″ deep, 29″ high, 12″ drop leaves. In Pennsylvania, **$350.**

Rosewood octagonal lift-top sewing stand with pedestal base and paw feet, 17″ wide, 17″ deep, 29″ high. In Texas, **$795.**

Close-up showing five lift-lid compartments in rosewood sewing stand.

Walnut oval table or tea ploy, 30″ wide, 20″ deep, 29″ high. In Virginia, **$165.**

Mahogany game table with pedestal base, paw and leaf metal feet; 38″ wide, 19″ deep, 29″ high. One of a pair of matching tables. In Virginia, **$1,000** the set.

The forerunner of current fold-up card tables was a stationary, usually fancy type, that could be made more compact by folding down its top. In this manner, a square surface became a rectangle, and the less common circular type formed a half circle. Sometimes these tables had an additional swinging leg, but frequently the top swiveled so that it was crosswise to the base. The top then could be opened to form a surface large enough to serve four.

Most of these tables could be arranged in three positions. First, since the top was hinged, it often was folded down upon itself to form a double surface. The top could be folded so that one half stood up against a wall, forming an appropriate backdrop for a statue, lamp or Christmas creche. The third position was the opened one, in which the top surface was extended to its fullest. Two examples with definite American Empire influences of the pre-1840s are illustrated. One has paw feet, and both the pedestal and the feet have carved leaves. The other has a cyma (a double curve) apron. These tables are called by a variety of names, including game, gaming, deal, or card.

Tip-top tables were space savers, too. Many were round, but others had straight lines or were octagonal. When a catch was released, they could be placed so that the top was vertical to the floor, not parallel to it. The table originally was developed to hold a tea service. Those with inlaid designs or pie-crust molding showed off their decorative touches well when the top was in a perpendicular position. One gentleman was offended by an early table of this type when he tried to arrange articles on its top, because the surface slanted slightly. This is a common complaint about the tables, which can slant with age. The tables now are referred to as tilt-top tables, since the terms tip or tip-up table are archaic.

A catalog by Nelson, Matter & Company, Manufacturers of Furniture, Grand Rapids, Michigan, in 1876 uses the word "center" (at time spelled "centre") instead of "parlor" in its copy on occasional tables. Terminology may differ, but the fact remains that these tables were used in the parlor and were available in many shapes, sizes, and with designs or legs that corresponded with the accepted style of furniture at the time. Both marble and wooden tops were available. Various tables were described as having serpentine tops, engraved legs (the current term is "incised"), carved and engraved legs, or heavy carved legs. Would you guess that a walnut center table with a serpentine wooden top, size 21½″ by 27″, might currently be called a turtle-top parlor table?

Bible stands sometimes had recessed tops, and their rims often were carved. The descriptions vary somewhat from those in use today, but then, so do the prices. A walnut or ash marble-top table with a serpentine outline, measuring 21″ by 27″, cost $10.25. Since laborers only earned a few cents an hour at that time, the table was expensive.

The exuberance of the Renaissance Revival can be seen on the base of an ebonized and gilt table. The recessed top has been temporarily covered, but should have a marble slab. Original floral roundels and gold engraved lines abound. It is stamped "C. F. Weber Furniture" under the frame. Since true ebony was a heavy tropical wood with a dense texture, it was easier to create an inexpensive substitute with a painted black coating. Eastlake styles include this imitation dark wood also. Rectangular tops were common in the late 1800s after the rococo curves of the mid-Victorian era were passé.

Returning to the rococo, a white marble turtle-top table shown in this chapter has a miniature dog carved at the base. Small scratches indicate that childish hands have patted him and swiveled him about. A close-up of a dog from another table shows the detailed work. Tables of this type have been found by the authors in Ohio, Illinois, and in the St. Louis, Missouri, area, but they are not common. The family piece shown left Madison, Indiana, for suburban Cleveland, Ohio, before it took up residency in South Carolina.

Some tables wore disguises. If you couldn't afford to buy one made from expensive, imported rosewood, why not pretend? Manufacturers were willing to help, as they applied artificial graining to walnut to make it look like

Walnut game table with cyma curve, mahogany veneer apron; 36″ wide, 18″ deep, 29″ high, 18″ drop leaf. In Indiana, **$400.**

Walnut tilt-top table with tripod pedestal base, 37″ diameter, 29″ high. In Indiana, **$425.**

rosewood. There were many ways to emulate rosewood's look, including special combs with rubber teeth or carefully designed rollers. Naturally, the rococo frame included exaggerated cyma curves. Pictured is a central finial that is pegged in place on the base shelf, becoming an urn filled with fruits, nuts, and leaves. The frame on the picture above the table is of real rosewood.

Coffee tables are not an 1800s concept; they belong to the twentieth century. When a housewife wants a "Victorian coffee table," she has to have a table cut down, much to the chagrin of the purist who would preserve it as is. Oval and rectangular parlor tables are used for this purpose, and library tables with generous proportions are occasionally selected for this treatment. Examples of cut-downs are pictured in this book.

Extension dining room tables were prevalent among mid-Victorian furniture. In earlier times, homeowners either owned a large table or formed one by joining smaller ones, especially those with drop leaves. The latter left the center of the room clear except at mealtime. Tables made to be joined were of the same height and width. Housewives were grateful for the development of extension tables requiring only one unit that opened up for leaves. Tables and stands of all sizes and shapes, both plain and intricate, were considered a necessity and certainly were present in almost every room of the Victorian house.

Walnut Renaissance Revival, Eastlake influence parlor table with applied roundels, burl veneer raised panels, incised lines, and ebonized and gilt decorations. "F. Weber Furniture" is stamped under replaced top. Original top was marble. 33″ wide, 23″ deep, 30″ high. In Missouri, **$450.**

Walnut turtle-top parlor table, 27″ wide, 22″ deep, 29″ high. In Illinois, **$260.** Parlor lamp, **$165.**

Walnut turtle-top center table with white marble, molded apron, and carved wooden dog that swivels on dowel pin; 36″ wide, 22″ deep, 29″ high. In South Carolina, **$900.**

Close-up of carved wooden dog on the base of another walnut parlor table.

Walnut Eastlake cut-down parlor table with gray marble top, incised lines, and burl banding; 29″ wide, 21″ deep, 17″ high. In Texas, **$250.**

Artificially grained rosewood on walnut turtle-top center table with white marble; molded apron; and urn with carved leaf, nuts, and fruit at base; 38″ wide, 24″ deep, 30″ high. In Texas, **$1,000.** Meissen lamp, 24″ high, **$350.** Wave Crest biscuit jar, 8″ high, **$250.** Rosewood frame, 19″ wide, 21″ high, **$150.**

Walnut pedestal extension table, 44″ wide, 44″ deep, 30″ high. In Iowa, **$1,250.**

Walnut lamp table, 14″ diameter, 25″ high. In Pennsylvania, **$150.**

Walnut "clover top" lamp table, 18″ wide, 18″ deep, 28″ high. In Ohio, **$165.**

Walnut Eastlake lamp table with incised lines, 16″ wide, 12″ deep, 31″ high. In Pennsylvania, **$100.**

Walnut lamp table with white marble top, incised lines, and applied roundels; 16″ diameter, 27″ high. In Illinois, **$400.**

Walnut Eastlake parlor table with rose marble top and incised lines, 19″ wide, 14″ deep, 28″ high. In Ohio, **$175.**

Walnut drop-leaf work table with pie crust beading on drawers, 20″ wide, 24″ deep, 30″ high, 9″ drop leaves. In Iowa, **$650.**

Walnut drop-leaf work table with spool legs, 18″ wide, 22″ deep, 30″ high. In Iowa, **$400.**

Walnut drop-leaf parlor table with pedestal base, 19″ wide, 33″ deep, 31″ high, 9″ drop leaves. In Iowa, **$650.**

Walnut drop-leaf work table, 20″ wide, 21″ deep, 29″ high, 9″ drop leaves. In Illinois, **$275.**

Walnut work table with chamfered drawer fronts, 21″ wide, 18″ deep, 28″ high. In Indiana, **$225.**

Walnut work table, 19″ wide, 16″ deep, 28″ high. In Indiana, **$210.**

Walnut sewing stand with lift top that reveals compartments for sewing needs. Veneered serpentine drawer front, fretwork, pull-out bin beneath drawer; 24″ wide, 16″ deep, 30″ high. In Texas, **$350.**

Walnut sewing table with applied decorations, burl veneer drawer panel, and pull-out bin beneath drawer; 24″ wide, 17″ deep, 29″ high. In Iowa, **$475.**

Walnut work table or night stand with sandwich pulls, 22″ wide, 16″ deep, 29″ high. In Pennsylvania, **$225.**

Walnut work table or night stand, 21″ wide, 17″ deep, 29″ high. In Ohio, **$160.** Blue-and-white bowl and pitcher from England, **$135.**

Walnut tilt-top table with tripod pedestal base, 31″ diameter, 29″ high. In Iowa **$350.**

Rosewood cut-down tilt-top table, 30″ diameter, 23″ high. In Texas, **$475.**

Walnut parlor table, 29″ diameter, 29″ high. In Ohio, **$225.**

Walnut-top parlor table with rosewood base, 29″ diameter, 30″ high. In Illinois, **$395.**

Walnut Eastlake table with marquetry top and incised lines, 22″ diameter, 29″ high. In Arkansas, **$300.**

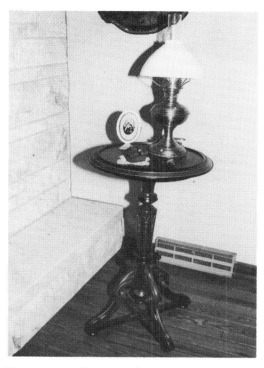

Walnut lamp table with incised lines, applied roundels, and gilt decorations; 20″ diameter, 33″ high. In Illinois, **$310.**

Walnut Eastlake parlor table with incised lines, 30″ wide, 22″ deep, 29″ high. In Illinois, **$210.**

Walnut Eastlake parlor table with incised lines, 30″ wide, 21″ deep, 29″ high. In Iowa, **$240.**

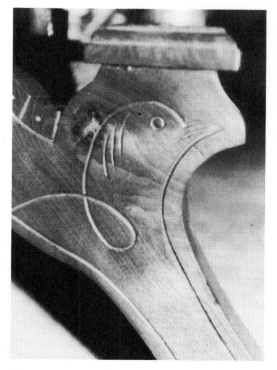

Close-up of incised bird's head on leg of Eastlake table.

Walnut parlor table with incised lines and applied roundels on apron, 29″ wide, 21″ deep, 29″ high. In Iowa, **$195.**

Walnut Eastlake parlor table with incised lines, 28″ wide, 19″ deep, 28″ high. In Illinois, **$245.**

Walnut Eastlake parlor table, 28″ wide, 22″ deep, 30″ high. In Pennsylvania, **$225.**

Walnut rococo parlor table with white marble top and mahogany apron, 31″ wide, 18″ deep, 28″ high. In Texas, **$585.**

Walnut parlor table with white marble top, incised lines, and molded apron; 30″ wide, 22″ deep, 29″ high. In Texas, **$800.** Original-condition kerosene lamp marked "France," with green thistle pattern and removable font to convert lamp to vase, 36″ high, **$750.**

Walnut Eastlake parlor table with white marble top, incised lines, applied roundels, burl veneer banding, and raised panels; 29″ wide, 20″ deep, 29″ high. In Texas, **$450.** Bradley and Hubbard lamp, 21″ high, **$295.** Wave Crest biscuit jar, 8½″ high to the finial, **$225.**

Walnut Eastlake parlor table with white marble top and incised lines, 30″ wide, 22″ deep, 29″ high. In Indiana, **$300.**

Walnut Eastlake parlor table with white marble top, incised lines, molded apron, and scalloped corners; 28″ wide, 20″ deep, 29″ high. In Ohio, **$400.**

Walnut Eastlake parlor table with white marble top and burl veneer panels, 32″ wide, 22″ deep, 29″ high. In Texas, **$375.** Bradley and Hubbard banquet lamp with pewter base, 27″ high, **$200.** Satin glass vase with gold enameled, decorated flowers on pink background, signed F (backwards) PK, 10″ high, **$225.**

Rosewood turtle-top center table with white marble top, serpentine aprons, and leaves carved on knees of legs; 41″ wide, 29″ deep, 27″ high. In Texas, **$1,750.** Opaque glass lamp, 34″ high, **$350.** French clock signed "Jacque Petite," circa 1810, with Romeo and Juliet bisque figures and porcelain base, **$1,850.**

Walnut turtle-top center table with reddish-brown marble, flame mahogany apron, and carved decorations on apron and legs; 38″ wide, 26″ deep, 30″ high. In Texas, **$1,500.**

Walnut parlor table with white marble, burl veneer panels on legs and apron, incised lines, and applied roundels; 28″ wide, 21″ deep, 30″ high. In Illinois, **$575.** Walnut clock with Minerva head at top, **$250.**

Walnut turtle-top center table with white marble top, veneered apron, and applied decorations; 36″ wide, 28″ deep, 30″ high. In Texas, **$650.**

Rosewood Renaissance Revival turtle-top center table with white marble top, carved decorations on apron and pedestal base; 41″ wide, 30″ deep, 30″ high. In Texas, **$2,000.** Tiffany paperweight, **$700.** Wave Crest ferner, 7″ diameter, 5″ high, **$500.** Burmese vase, 6″ wide, 4″ deep, 8″ high, **$900.**

Rosewood turtle-top center table with white marble top, grotesques for legs, and carved decorations; 36″ wide, 28″ deep, 30″ high. In Texas, **$1,000.**

Walnut turtle-top center table with white marble top and applied decorations on veneered apron, 30″ wide, 19″ deep, 30″ high. In Texas, **$650.** Walnut oval frame with mirror, 18″ wide, 21″ high, **$100.**

Rosewood center table with white marble top and ornately decorated pedestal, 37″ wide, 29″ deep, 29″ high. In Missouri, **$1,200.**

Walnut Renaissance Revival center table with white marble top, incised and applied decorations on apron, and urn at center of base; 36″ wide, 28″ deep, 28″ high. In Illinois, **$850.** Parlor lamp, 23″ high, **$275.** Walnut footstools, 20″ wide, 17″ deep, 14″ high, **$185** each.

Rosewood turtle-top table with ornately carved base, 54″ wide, 34″ deep, 30″ high. In Texas, **$2,000.**

Walnut cut-down parlor table with white marble top, incised lines, and applied decorations; 32″ wide, 24″ deep, 24″ high. In Pennsylvania, **$450.**

Walnut cut-down parlor table with white marble top, applied roundels and decorations; 32″ wide, 24″ deep, 23″ high. In Illinois, **$500.**

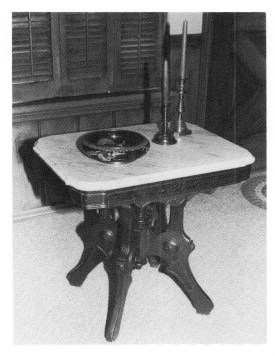

Walnut Eastlake cut-down parlor table with white marble top, incised lines, and applied roundels; 24″ wide, 19″ deep, 23″ high. In Texas, **$250.**

Walnut Eastlake cut-down parlor table with brown marble top, incised lines, and applied roundels; 30″ wide, 21″ deep, 19″ high. In Texas, **$250.**

Walnut Renaissance Revival cut-down library table; 48″ wide, 28″ deep, 20″ high. In Texas, **$600.**

Walnut extension dining table, 41″ wide, 29″ deep, 29″ high. In Illinois, **$295.**

Walnut pedestal extension table, 45″ diameter, 30″ high. In Illinois, **$1,385.** Cane seat chair with burl design on splat back, 35″ high, **$175** each in a set of six.

Walnut pedestal extension table with applied roundels and molded legs, 47" diameter, 29" high. In Iowa, **$1,500.**

Mahogany pedestal extension table with carved base, ball and claw feet, and five leaves; 54" diameter, 30" high. In Texas, **$1,850.**

Walnut pedestal dining table with applied roundels and decorations, 45" diameter, 29" high. In Iowa, **$1,200.**

Walnut three-legged dining table with burl veneer apron, 40″ diameter, 31″ high. In Illinois, **$275.**

Cherry dining table, 40″ diameter, 30″ high. In Iowa, **$400.**

Cherry extension dining table with two leaves, 44″ diameter, 30″ high. In Pennsylvania, **$395.**

Cherry drop-leaf dining table with spool legs, 41″ wide, 21″ deep, 30″ high, 14″ drop leaves. In Pennsylvania, **$450.**

Walnut drop-leaf dining table with gate (or swing) leg, 42″ wide, 21″ deep, 30″ high, 18″ drop leaves. In Texas, **$700.**

Walnut drop-leaf dining table with scalloped drop leaves, 42″ wide, 25″ deep, 29″ high, 18″ drop leaves. In Illinois, **$950.**

5

Store It Here

In rustic homes, a few hooks on the wall and homemade cupboards held a family's possessions. On the other extreme, wealthy people furnished their dwellings with mahogany, walnut, or rosewood furniture from Europe or that made by quality craftsmen in the United States. When the factory system helped create a larger middle class and made mass-produced products available, family's furnishings increased as their wants expanded.

Whatnots were sold to hold bric-a-brac. Some had four or five graduated shelves and stood in the corner, while others stood flush against the wall. Women who wanted to be especially stylish called them by their French name — étagères. (Today many people reserve that term for the large, fancy whatnots with mirrors.) Some étagères featured a central drawer and a slab of marble. An unsual type, known as a closed étagère, has an open top, but the base has doors with glass panes. Applied carvings, pierced work, finials, burl panels, and turned supports were used to decorate these impressive pieces of furniture.

Sideboards frequently were a center of attraction in the dining room. They held linens, silver, and china. Their styles reflected the current trends, as the soft, rounded lines of rococo changed to the straighter look of the Renaissance and gave way to the Eastlake boxy look. Sideboards are also known as buffets. In dining rooms without a sideboard, a cupboard sometimes was substituted.

Kitchen cupboards customarily were more rustic than those that graced the dining room. One type with punched-tin panels was called a pie safe because it was used to protect baked goods from flies and mice, who like sweets as much as we do. The pierced-tin panels on the front and sides of the safes were too tough for a rodent's sharp, gnawing teeth to penetrate, yet they let air circulate in the cupboard to retard molding and help keep the pies edible.

These represent a few of the storage units found in the dining and kitchen areas of the Victorian house. Built-ins replaced kitchen cupboards in the twentieth century.

Walnut side whatnot with fretwork, 32″ wide and 12″ deep at base, 56″ high. In Illinois, **$245.**

Walnut side whatnot, 57″ high graduates from 33″ wide, 12″ deep at base to 26″ wide, 8″ deep at top. In Texas, **$385.**

Rosewood closed étagère with applied carvings on drawer and chamfered stiles, mirror in back of two top shelves, cupboard base with glass doors; 42″ wide, 20″ deep, 80″ high. In Texas, **$3,000.**

Walnut corner whatnot with scalloped outline on shelves and uprights, 25″ wide, 18″ deep, 60″ high. In Illinois, **$275.**

Walnut corner whatnot, 53″ high, graduates from 21″ wide, 14″ deep at base to 13″ wide, 9″ deep at top. In Illinois, **$265.**

Walnut étagère with white marble over hidden drawer and an undecipherable label from a Boston maker; 49″ wide, 15″ deep, 84″ high. In Missouri, **$2,500.**

Walnut étagère grained to resemble rosewood, by Mitchells and Rammelsberg, Cincinnati, Ohio, Manufacturers; 53″ wide, 15″ deep, 86″ high. In Illinois, **$2,500.**

Walnut rococo étagère with full drawer, mirror back; 65″ wide, 14″ deep, 80″ high. In Arkansas, **$2,000.** Wave Crest items in collection on shelf above drawer range in value from **$175** to **$1,000.** Pitchers at the base, from left to right, are coin spot, fern and daisy, coin spot, coin spot, and hobnail.

Walnut side whatnot has middle drawer with no handles, 43″ wide, 15″ deep at base, 74″ high. In Texas, **$450.**

Walnut china cabinet with serpentine glass sides and door, French legs, beading at top; 36″ wide, 15″ deep, 61″ high. In Virginia, **$900.**

Walnut Renaissance Revival étagère with white marble top above drawer, central mirror and burl panels; 47″ wide, 16″ deep, 92″ high. In Illinois, **$3,200.**

Walnut étagère with center mirror, molded pediment with applied decorations, and white marble over base drawer, 48″ wide, 15″ deep, 13″ to marble, 89″ above marble. In Illinois, **$2,800.**

Rosewood rococo closed étagère or sideboard with applied carvings, pierced gallery and beading; 48″ wide, 22″ deep, 72″ high. In Illinois, **$2,200.**

Walnut étagère with galleries that flank beveled mirror, applied roundels, and incised lines; 47″ wide, 15″ deep, 69″ high. In Texas, **$1,500.**

Walnut rococo sideboard with white marble top, applied leaf and nut carvings, and circular molding on doors; 56″ wide, 21″ deep, 82″ high. In Texas, **$2,250.**

Close-up of leaf and nut carving on walnut rococo sideboard.

Walnut Renaissance Revival sideboard, with carved fish and birds in door panels, white marble top; 48″ wide, 19″ deep, 91″ high. In Illinois, **$2,250.**

Chestnut Renaissance Revival sideboard with applied carvings, molded panels, and white marble top; 54″ wide, 21″ deep, 76″ high. In Illinois, **$1,995.**

Walnut Renaissance Revival sideboard with white marble top, applied carvings on door panels, and carved head below pediment; 54″ wide, 22″ deep, 87″ high. In Illinois, **$2,200.**

Walnut Renaissance Revival sideboard with marble top, burl panels, and applied decorations; 42″ wide, 20″ deep, 76″ high. In Texas, **$1,800.**

Maple and chestnut sideboard with burl panels on molded doors, and white marble top; 54″ wide, 23″ deep, 56″ high. In Pennsylvania, **$950.**

Walnut sideboard (sometimes referred to as a chiffonier in England) with ebony and gilt pulls (teardrops), burl panels, and incised lines; 37″ wide, 18″ deep, 55″ high. In Texas, **$750.**

Walnut sideboard with pink marble top, Circassian walnut veneer, applied and carved sheaf of grain with farm tools in top center panel, and applied decorations; 62″ wide, 22″ deep, 85″ high. In Iowa, **$5,000.**

Walnut Eastlake sideboard with incised lines, burl panels and brass handles; 42″ wide, 20″ deep, 76″ high. In Texas, **$1,500.** On top shelf, left to right: Bennington pitcher, 10″ high, **$75.** European brass tea kettle, **$100.** European rosewood bombay coffee grinder, **$200.** In enclosed cupboard: German bowl, **$85.** German cake plate, **$85.** On marble top: ruby thumbprint castor set, compote, spooner, and pitcher; **$300** the whole set.

Walnut sideboard with burl veneer, arched mirrors, beading, and scalloped white marble top; 58″ wide, 20″ deep, 31″ high. In Illinois, **$1,500.**

Cherry buffet with applied decorations on chamfered stiles, beading on apron; 60″ wide, 19″ deep, 42″ high. In Iowa, **$1,400.**

Walnut step-back cupboard with pie shelf and arched, molded door panels; 46″ wide, 18″ deep, 83″ high. In Indiana, **$595.**

Walnut cupboard, 52″ wide, 13″ deep, 86″ high. In Indiana, **$995.**

Walnut pie safe with six punched-tin panels, 37″ wide, 18″ deep 57″ high. In Illinois, **$435.**

Walnut cupboard, 43″ wide, 16″ deep, 65″ high. In Illinois, **$1,065.**

6

This Is the Library

A library in a home? Many houses included such a room. In more modest abodes, furniture that held writing supplies, books, or magazines was assigned to the most convenient space. Since desks were usually both functional and attractive, they held a place of prominence. Today a fine secretary of yesteryear is impressive enough to be the focal point of a room.

An 1876 catalog uses the term "fall leaf" to describe a slant front that drops down to form the writing surface on a desk. Today such hinged lids are referred to as drop- or fall-front types. When opened, the fall leaf is supported by a chain attached to the body of the piece or by pull-out brackets or slides on either side.

It is strange that desks were simply portable boxes prior to the late 1600s. Through the process of evolution, many styles emerged. The change began when someone decided to support the box on a stand-like frame. From then on, cabinetmakers continued to change the structure to make it more convenient. A space eventually was created for a person's legs. And someone decided to slant the top and attach a hinged lid that opened up away from the user. Inside the box were the needed supplies, including a quill pen, ink bottle, paper, and sand, which was sprinkled over the writing to dry the ink. When the hinges were attached at the front so that a slanting leaf could be pulled down, desks became more convenient. The inside was outfitted with compartments called pigeonholes, and when drawers were added, a full-grown desk emerged. Desks with bookcase tops, known as secretaries, had larger storage areas. Their designs and outlines changed with the times, but they remained impressive and functional.

Walnut slant-front desk with burl veneer raised panel on drop front, 45″ wide, 20″ deep, 38″ high. In Indiana, **$750.**

Walnut lift-top desk with incised lines, burl veneer raised panels on drawers, and recessed veneered panel beneath gallery shelf; 27″ wide, 21″ deep, 50″ high. In Illinois, **$900.**

Walnut slant-front secretary with applied decorations and circular molding on slant front, 40″ wide, 21″ deep, 90″ high. In Texas, **$3,500.**

Walnut Eastlake cylinder-front secretary with spoon carving; incised lines; and burl veneer panels on cylinder, doors, and drawers; 39″ wide, 22″ deep, 84″ high. In Illinois, **$2,800.**

A fall-front desk that has a table base and full-length drawer now is known as a Lincoln desk, named for the president. This style was manufactured for many years. Undoubtedly, when Honest Abe was a circuit-riding lawyer in the 1850s, he used such desks. The style outlived Mr. Lincoln. In the late 1870s, a catalog listing for a Lincoln desk refers to it as a hinged cornice desk, since the top could be raised, revealing what was almost a secret compartment. The catalog also unimaginatively described a "fall leaf desk with table." Today it might be called a student desk.

"I'd like to find a large cylinder desk so that I could pull the top down to hide all my papers when I'm not using it," said a businessman. Of course, he wanted to purchase one for much less than the current prices. Cylinder deks have a quarter-round front that rolls down to cover the writing surface and pigeonholes when the desk is not in use. Beneath are drawers and possibly a cupboard. When a glass-enclosed bookcase is placed on top, the desk becomes a cylinder secretary. The cylinder desk differs from a roll-top desk, which has a flexible hood, or *tambour*, that slides down as a rounded lid. This hood is formed by a series of narrow horizontal strips of wood, which usually are glued to a strong fabric backing. The bases of desks with these sliding covers contain drawers alone, or a combination of a cupboard and drawers. When an enclosed bookcase top is added, a secretary desk is created.

What connection is there between a davenport desk and a ship captain's version? Usually they are both small and, in most examples, the drawers slide out at one side. The term "davenport" is used in England, where these desks might serve in the nursery, one per child. Most versions seem to have slant fronts, called "book slides" in early catalogs. The lids are hinged at the back and lift up to expose a storage area within. One side of the piece may have fake drawer fronts so that both ends are symetrical.

Walnut fall-front table desk with gallery, 37″ wide, 23″ deep, 30″ high, 7″ gallery. In Virginia, **$850.**

Walnut lift-top davenport desk with burl veneer raised panels and carved woman's head on gallery, two doors in the front rather than on the side; 28″ wide, 21″ deep, 39″ high at the back. In Illinois, **$1,200.**

A desk that looks as if it is pregnant was developed by William S. Wooten and is called by his name. Its two half-barrel divisions meet in the middle of the front and swing open to expose about one hundred compartments for papers or ledger books. It is so compact that one scarcely has to move in order to reach any papers. The Wooten desks had one lock, a metal-lined slot that served as a mail or bill drop writing surface. Convenience was the key. Pictured is a Renaissance Revival "Wooten Patent Cabinet Office Secretary" that was manufactured from the 1870s to 1880s, mainly in Indianapolis but later in Danville. Mr. Wooten was a leader in the Society of Friends and sometimes was referred to as Reverend. Sundays were reserved for worship — no cooking or recreation allowed. The Friends couldn't play cards as gamblers did, but Flinch, a simple mathematical game in which a player tried to get rid of his numbered cards by building piles up from one or down from fifteen was considered safe. Wooten

desks currently are popular and again perform their useful function. Wooten's company made school furniture and a patented rotary desk, as well. Different grades and designs of the various types were manufactured.

Another patented piece could be considered a bed, a fall-front desk, or a secretary, because it is all of these. It contains a coil spring and feather ticking, making the bed complete when it is open. The label reads, "Eaton Ware Mattress Company, Chicago, Ill. Sole Mft." The patent dates are April 24, 1884, June 2, 1885, and July 7, 1885. Obviously this combination piece required a generous space in order to function properly. It is doubtful that it was made in quantities. Has anyone ever seen one to match it?

Another library item that would be equally at home in the parlor was a canterbury, whose primary function now is to hold magazines. Its name evolved because a clergyman wanted a portable stand that could hold sheets of music

Walnut Wooten desk with applied decorations, burl veneer raised panels, applied molding framing the veneer panels, and incised lines; 40″ wide, 27″ deep, 66″ high. In Texas, **$10,000.**

A view of the inside of a Wooten desk.

or other items. Since Canterbury was a religious site in England, the name seemed appropriate. Some canterburys were designed to transport a tray with cutlery and supper plates, but this original use is ignored today.

In addition to the bookcases that formed the top of secretary desks, there were free-standing forms of various sizes and ornamentations. Generally, these bookcases had two doors with glass panes, and a drawer or two was incorporated at the base.

Walnut canterbury with fretwork and one drawer, 22″ wide, 11″ deep, 35″ high. In Illinois, **$450.**

Walnut bed desk with burl veneer panels in open position.

Walnut bed desk showing the slant-front secretary base that also functions as the bed's footboard.

Walnut bed desk in closed position as a slant-front secretary. A label reads: "Eaton Ware Mattress Company, Chicago, Ill. Sole Mft. April 24, 1884, June 2, 1885, July 7, 1885;" 60″ wide, 90″ high. In Iowa, unpriced.

Walnut rolltop desk with étagère top showing applied decorations, twisted and molded shelf supports, burl veneer raised panels, and brass bas relief figural plaques; 34″ wide, 23″ deep, 62″ high. In Illinois, **$3,450.**

Walnut slant-front desk with beading on slant front and drawer, applied decorations; 45″ wide, 20″ deep, 43″ high. In Ohio, **$1,000.**

Walnut drop-front table secretary with ebony and gilt pulls (teardrops) on drawer, 41″ wide, 22″ deep, 89″ high. In Texas, **$2,500.**

Cherry secretary with fold-out writing surface, 52″ wide, 22″ deep, 90″ high. In Illinois, **$2,200.**

Walnut secretary with fold-out writing surface, applied decorations, recessed drawer panels, and projection front, 42″ wide, 22″ deep, 89″ high. In Illinois, **$2,150.**

Walnut stained slant-front secretary with applied decorations on cornice, artificially grained burl veneer panels on drawers; 39″ wide, 18″ deep, 87″ high. In Iowa, **$950.**

Walnut Eastlake slant-front secretary with incised lines, pierced railing cornice; 35″ wide, 19″ deep, 87″ high. In Illinois, **$1,650.**

Walnut Eastlake slant-front secretary with incised lines, applied decorations, burl veneer raised panels on bookcase top, and burl veneer banding on doors and drawers; 39″ wide, 21″ deep, 88″ high. In Texas, **$1,650.**

Walnut fall-front table desk with burl veneer raised panel on fall front, veneer on drawer; 27″ wide, 19″ deep, 55″ high. In Ohio, **$625.**

Walnut fall-front desk with applied roundels, burl veneer raised panel on fall front, molding bands framing door panels, and one shelf gallery; 26″ wide, 16″ deep, 61″ high. In South Carolina, **$750.**

Walnut and rosewood fall-front desk with incised lines, applied decorations, rosewood burl raised panels, ebony and gilt pulls (teardrop), drop-front compartment beneath drawer, and bookshelf at base; 37″ wide, 18″ deep, 72″ high. In Texas, **$2,000.**

Walnut Eastlake lift-top desk with incised lines, applied decorations, and burl veneer banding; 36″ wide, 22″ deep, 30″ high. In Illinois, **$350.**

Walnut fall-front desk with applied decorations; molding bands framing the fall front, drawer, and door panels; and burl veneer raised panels; 34″ wide, 18″ deep, 52″ high. In Illinois, **$1,050.**

Walnut fall-front desk with burl veneer banding and panels, incised lines, top gallery with inscribed and molded decorations, open shelf between drawer and lower doors for books or storage, and a shelf at each side to hold candles or oil lamps; 28″ wide, 16″ deep, 54″ high. In Texas, **$800.** Royal Bonn clock from Germany with red roses, **$400.**

Walnut fall-front desk with molded burl veneer raised panels, molded door and fall-front frames, and one shelf gallery; 30″ wide, 17″ deep, 71″ high. In Pennsylvania, **$750.**

Walnut table desk, 36″ wide, 20″ deep, 76″ high. In Alabama, **$850.**

Walnut étagère desk with pull-out writing surface above drawer, dated April 26, 1870; 37″ wide, 14″ deep, 65″ high. In Iowa, **$700.**

Walnut étagère desk with fall-front secretary drawer, and applied decorations; 38″ wide, 18″ deep, 73″ high. In Texas, **$850.**

Walnut cylinder-front desk with projection front; burl veneer raised panels; and veneer on cylinder, drawer, and door panels; 39″ wide, 21″ deep, 43″ high. In Wisconsin, **$2,195.**

Walnut cylinder-front secretary with burl veneer pilasters; burl veneer banding on cornice, drawer front, and door panels; 45″ wide, 21″ deep, 83″ high. In Texas, **$1,800.**

Walnut cylinder-front secretary with applied roundels and pilasters; burl veneer raised panels; and burl veneer on cylinder, drawer, and door fronts; 41″ wide, 23″ deep, 84″ high. In Pennsylvania, **$1,700.**

Walnut Eastlake cylinder-front secretary with a pierced cornice, burl veneer panels; 35″ wide, 23″ deep, 85″ high. In Missouri, **$1,700.**

Walnut cylinder-front secretary with molded burl veneer paneled cornice, circular molding, and burl veneer raised panels on drawers; 42″ wide, 22″ deep, 99″ high. In South Carolina, **$2,400.**

Walnut canterbury (or magazine rack) with fretwork and push-through drawer, 22″ wide, 14″ deep, 24″ high. In Arkansas, **$450.**

Walnut Eastlake cylinder-front secretary with incised lines, projection front, and burl veneer panels; 41″ wide, 22″ deep, 92″ high. In Texas, **$2,500.**

Walnut lift-top davenport desk with lift-lid storage compartment on top, burl veneer, four working drawers on the right-hand side, and four fake drawers on the opposite side; 22″ wide, 18″ deep at top, 31″ high. In Illinois, **$700.**

Continued on page 105

Walnut parlor table with white marble insert and hand-carved dog at base, 35″ wide, 26″ deep, 29″ high. In Illinois, **$1,050.** China clocks in background range from **$325** to **$365.** Parlor lamp on table, 29″ high, **$685.**

Walnut cylinder-front davenport desk with Circassian walnut veneer on cylinder, door, and front panels, and applied veneer panels and Minerva head on gallery; 26″ wide, 24″ deep, 46″ high. In Illinois, **$1,650.** Walnut shadow box above desk with feather flowers, 17″ wide, 6″ deep, 19″ high, **$165.**

Walnut étagère with pierced, carved pediment and white marble over drawer, 48″ wide, 18″ deep, 90″ high. In Arkansas, **$2,500.** Left to right, top to bottom: Six-sided American Beauty diamond-quilted vase with applied rim, 8″ high, **$300.** Webb peach blow enameled vase, 8″ high, **$400.** Webb blue peach blow vase, 10″ high, **$500.** Pair of mother-of-pearl diamond-quilted rose bowls, 5″ diameter, 2″ high, **$400.** Webb blue peach blow vase, 10″ high, **$500.** Mother-of-pearl diamond quilted ewer, 13″ high, **$500.** Cased satin glass vase with applied feet, 9″ high (matching vase on opposite shelf), **$400** the pair. Mother-of-pearl diamond-quilted vase, 9″ high (matching vase on opposite shelf), **$1,000** the pair. Matched pair of enameled bristol vases, 14″ high, **$400.**

Rosewood étagère attributed to Prudent Mallard, with molded and carved pediment, pierced carving, finials, white marble top, and mirror on cupboard door; 58″ wide, 18″ deep, 95″ high. In Missouri, **$4,500.** Banquet lamp with ribbed shade, coin spot mother-of-pearl satin glass font, and brass base, **$1,000.**

Rosewood rococo étagère with pierced and applied carving, mirrored door and back, and galleried revolving side compartments that are locked by turning the turrets; 61″ wide, 22″ deep, 80″ high. In Illinois, **$2,700.**

Walnut oval center table with white marble top, 38″ wide, 29″ deep, 31″ high. In Texas, **$1,200.** Hobnail cranberry pitcher, 8″ high, **$300.** Female figure metal electric lamp with cut-glass beaded shades made in Paris, 29″ high, **$400.** Stevens and Williams tree-trunk-shaped pitcher with blue handle, 10″ high, **$225.**

Walnut common washstand, 29″ wide, 14″ deep, 29″ to the top with a 5″ back. In Iowa, **$225.** Brass lamp with new shade, **$189.**

Rosewood framed fire screen with beaded needle-point insert of flowers and rough-cut wool cockatoo. Baudouine or Mallard characteristics. 34″ wide, 19″ deep at base, 49″ high. In Missouri, **$1,250.**

Walnut commode washstand with gray fossilized marble top and splashback, incised lines, ebony decoration, burl veneer on splashback frame and top drawer, and burl veneer facing on two small drawers and door; 36″ wide, 20″ deep, 44″ high. In Texas, **$450.** Aladdin Lincoln Drape lamp with original painted shade, 24″ high, **$225.** Mt. Washington shell and seaweed biscuit jar, 8″ high, **$350.**

Walnut somnoe or half-commode with white marble top and applied circular molding on drawer and door, 19″ wide, 16″ deep, 30″ high. In Illinois, **$550.** Two 7″ Steiff bears, circa 1907, **$400** each. Steiff bear, 12″, circa 1910, **$450.** Parker fountain pen, 9″, circa 1910, **$750.** Waterman #20 fountain pen, 9″, circa 1910, **$1,000.** Unmarked Shirley Temple doll and circa 1930s Lenci boy doll.

Rosewood Jelliff sofa with male warrior heads as arm supports, metal medallion warrior's head on crest, and drop finials; 79″ wide, 44″ high. A gentleman's chair and side chair complete the three-piece set. In Texas, **$5,000** for the three pieces.

Walnut commode washstand with applied drawer panels, molded door panels, and applied decorations on chamfered stiles; 31″ wide, 16″ deep, 30″ high. In Illinois, **$325.**

Victorian parlor showing a Belter rosewood Rosalie gentleman's and lady's chair with rose and grape carved crests. In Illinois, **$2,500** each. Rosewood center table with white marble top and carved birds' heads on pedestal, 29″ diameter, 28″ high. **$1,300.**

Illinois antiques shop scene showing walnut parlor tables ranging in price from **$495** to **$785**, and table and hanging lamps ranging in price from **$225** to **$595.**

Walnut Renaissance Revival armchairs with incised lines, molded and carved crest, burl veneer raised panels, and button-tufted backs; 29″ arm to arm, 43″ high. In Missouri, **$900** the pair. Walnut copper-lined pedestal base planter with incised lines, drop finials, and two porcelain panels depicting a stork and an owl on the "night" side. The "day" side shows a toucan and the bird of paradise. A grosse and a falcon are on the ends; 22″ wide, 13″ deep, 44″ high. **$1,000.**

Rosewood love seat with button-tufted medallion back and rose carved, pierced crest, 45″ arm to arm, 44″ high. In Texas, **$2,250.**

Walnut bookcase with incised lines, applied roundels, and burl veneer panels; 40″ wide, 14″ deep at base, 12″ deep at top, 59″ high. In Missouri, **$500.**

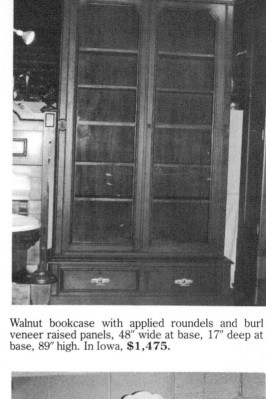

Walnut bookcase with applied roundels and burl veneer raised panels, 48″ wide at base, 17″ deep at base, 89″ high. In Iowa, **$1,475.**

Walnut bookcase with burl veneer pilasters and raised panels, 44″ wide, 14″ deep, 90″ high. In Illinois, **$1,395.**

Walnut bookcase with incised lines and applied decorations, 42″ wide, 13″ deep, 70″ high. In Illinois, **$875.**

7

We Bought a Bedchamber Suite

How exciting it must have been for a bride of the mid-1800s to exclaim, "We bought a bedchamber suite." A young wife of the early 1800s would not have uttered those words, because matching sets weren't available then.

Before indoor plumbing, pitchers and bowls were common in the bedroom. A wealthy family might have a storage tank for rainwater in the attic, with pipes leading to a room with a large metal tub. Servants added heated water so that the tub temperature would be comfortable. Less affluent people dragged a tub to the middle of the kitchen floor, and each member of the family had a turn at taking a Saturday night bath. Since water from the outdoor pump could be mighty cold at certain times of the year, it was heated on the stove to provide a fresh supply for each bather. For quicker clean-up jobs, a family used bedroom washstands that usually consisted of a top with one drawer, towel bar ends, and a bottom shelf for a wash bowl and pitcher.

A commode washstand was more dignified and decorative. It offered various combinations of drawers and doors, with storage shelves inside. Carved handles and applied decorations, moldings, burl veneer panels, and gently curving back rails lent these commodes a personality of their own. Some had ebony and gilt pulls, now called teardrops. The brass back plates on them can be cleaned, but the black wooden drop should be untouched to emulate ebony. Small shelves on the splashback held the soap dish or an oil lamp or a candle. Factories offered a choice of woods; it cost approximately fifty cents more to purchase walnut instead of the light-colored ash or chestnut.

A lift-top commode washstand was just that. The top was hinged to lift, revealing a step arrangement inside. The bowl occupied the top position, and the tall pitcher rested on the lower level. Sometimes water rings on the inside shelves are evidence that two damp pieces were used for many years. Washstands with a marble top cost a dollar extra. The back rails have been removed from many of these commode washstands, perhaps to modernize them or to make them fit into a special space, such as under the eves in an upstairs room. The washstands are, of course, more expensive when they are complete.

Commode washstand with burl panels, ebony and gilt pulls (teardrops); 32″ wide, 15″ deep, 30″ to top, back rail 8″. In Iowa, **$475.**

Common washstand with spool turned legs, 20″ wide, 15″ deep, 28″ high. In Connecticut, **$95.** Oak comb case with pressed design, towel bar, and mirror; 17″ wide, 17″ high, **$45.**

Walnut lift-top commode washstand with top that lifts to store wash bowl and pitcher, 30″ wide, 18″ deep, 30″ high. In Indiana, **$350.**

Walnut veneered somnoe with white marble top, projection drawer, and applied carvings; 19″ wide, 17″ deep, 29″ high. In Arkansas, **$750.** White satin glass, mother of pearl, diamond-quilted lamp, **$900.**

How would you like to own a half commode? These actually are considered choice since they are not found as often as their larger sisters. The catalog term for such a piece is *somnoe*. With their one drawer and cupboard space beneath, they work well as stands beside modern beds since they no longer have to be cluttered with bowls, pitchers, and towels.

Bureau washstands are small chests, usually with three drawers. Some have two small parallel drawers at the top and two full-length beneath. A retractable rod sometimes was situated at the side to accommodate towels and washcloths. Notice the wide variety of hardware on the examples shown. Hardware includes handles, (even when they are not of metal), escutcheons (keyhole outlines), and hinges. It cost less to purchase unfinished furniture that did not have handles. A skillful person could supply his own pulls and apply his own varnish. That's one reason there is such a variation. For people with less talent or more money, the completed product was available.

Many people probably thought that unfinished furniture that could be painted or stained as desired was a novel merchandising idea. Back then, unfinished pieces were referred to as "in white." The current term, "naked" furniture, would shock the prim Victorian ladies.

One convenient deviation from the normal bureau washstand had what are referred to as towel bar ends. But when a stand did not provide a place for towels, a special rack or towel horse could be purchased. Sturdier, stouter versions were quilt racks, on which extra bed covers were kept available. It was a matter of pride to show off needlework — especially when a semstress developed her own design variations. Quilts given to brides and old friends represented fond memories and might be folded carefully over a quilt rack.

To the French, a bureau is a desk, but in the United States, a bureau is a chest of drawers. An ash bedroom suite that included a bed, bureau, and matching washstand was offered at the low price of twenty dollars, providing it was "in white, no marble, no pulls and no plate." That's like buying a car with no air conditioning, no heater, no radio, and no extras. "In white" meant unfinished, and "no plate" indicated that there was no mirror included. If you splurged and spent an extra dollar, you could buy the set "in white with marble and pulls. No plate." A "plate" cost one dollar and seventy five cents, with an added charge of two dollars to apply the finish to the frame. When the whole suite was "finished Complete," it cost twenty-seven dollars. To a worker who labored for a few dollars a week, the set was costly. The options that helped reduce the expense must have seemed attractive.

A chest of drawers without an attached mirror is shown. An interesting portrait of a gentleman, the owner's ancestor, hangs over it. The suit he wears was prepainted on the canvas, then the subject's face was added. It is said that itinerant painters earned cash plus their room and board for such portraits. In stretches of inclement weather, they drew headless busts upon which they could sketch a patron's likeness when fair weather permitted them to roam once more.

In the 1800s, "toilet" referred to personal grooming, and a mirror was called a toilet or plate. Do you know what a deck is? The two small drawers that sit across from each other on the top of a bureau were called decks during the 1870s. They are now known as handkerchief boxes. Much less common were the petite boxes with hinged lift lids that sat on top of the dresser. An oval "plate" is now called a wishbone mirror, since the frame in which it is suspended is shaped roughly like a fowl's wishbone.

A projection front refers to the part of a dresser that hangs out over the base. A drawer or two may project or overhang the others. Slipper drawers had no handles and appeared to be the apron on a dresser. Not surprisingly, they were used for slippers. On some dressers, there were hidden compartments for jewelry.

Suites with dressing cases from the Victorian period were more expensive than the bureau type, and more elegant as well. Sometimes their tall mirrors seemed to extend from floor to ceiling and had ornately carved frames

Walnut bureau washstand with white marble top, leaf escutcheons, and burl panels; 31″ wide, 17″ deep, 29″ high. In Indiana, **$425.**

Walnut bureau washstand with towel bar ends, 32″ wide, 18″ deep, 29″ high. In Indiana, **$400.**

that featured small bracket shelves for candle-holders or small lamps. Drawers varied in number and size. What is now described as a well or step-down generally separated the parallel series of drawers. All three levels were treated alike, with either wooden or marble tops. At the bottom were full-length drawers. The mid-section below the looking glass often went down to the floor level, but this was not a common arrangement. To achieve individuality, you could order your own mirror ("toilet") frame or select from sixteen different carved pulls.

A chiffonier is a tall, narrow chest of drawers. A nineteenth-century catalog states, "Cheffoniers (note the "che"), walnut... six drawers, one lock secures all." The spelling may be a proofreader's error, because the company also offered East Lake styles. English furniture designer Charles Eastlake might have expressed surprise at this division of his name. At any rate, the chiffoniers described are now called sidelocks, since their left stiles open when the key is turned. When the stile is closed, all of the drawers lock with one twist of the key.

While twin beds did not exist as such during the 1800s, there were single sizes manufactured. It was not until the 1900s that a bed duet was dubbed "twin," so a buyer should be wary if he is offered identical "antique" twin beds. It is possible they could be cut-down versions of larger ones. Any part of the chamber furniture was available alone. A three-quarter-size bed was the norm, but double types were common too. Today it is possible to have a smaller mattress made when an antique bed is not large enough to accommodate a ready-made version. But because today's tall people prefer to sprawl out over a larger surface, you might add length by substituting metal side rails for the wooden ones. With these, a standard mattress will usually function well. Hold on to the wooden rails so you can restore the bed to its original size if desired. The two- and three-piece bedroom sets in the photographs range from rococo to Renaissance and Eastlake in style.

When closets were not built into homes, families needed furniture in which to hang their garments. Tall, wide wardrobes were the answer, but for those with a desire to emulate the

Walnut quilt rack with Gothic feel, 25″ long, 35″ high. In Illinois, **$225.**

Walnut four-drawer chest with circular molding, 39″ wide, 18″ deep, 37″ high. In Texas, **$350.** Banquet lamp, 26″ high, **$450.** Double frame, 31″ wide, 34″ high. **$125.** (Man's head was added to pre-painted figure.)

French, the name was armoire (originally a cupboard where unwieldly armor was stored). Many included a partition with shelves and a deep drawer on one side with a space for hanging garments on the other. There could be one or two drawers at the base.

Wardrobes refuse to bend when going around corners and often are impossible to move up narrow stairways. Some ingenious craftsmen decided to make theirs with removable pegs so that the cases could be completely disassembled. This solved the moving problems. The sides, doors, back, top, and shelves were carried in separate pieces. One word of warning, however: mark each part with numbers and arrows to indicate where it fits. Without this, the reassembling can be tricky. Today these wardrobes report for duty in almost any room in the home, including the parlor. In fact, all of the various washstands and dressers have been promoted from the bedchamber to other rooms, but the bed itself maintains its proper place in the bedchamber. Some things never change.

Walnut dresser with wishbone mirror, two decks, and molded drawer panels; 42″ wide, 18″ deep, 71″ high. In Texas, **$750.**

Walnut chiffonier (also called sidelock) with hinged stile locks, burl veneer panels on stiles and drawers, and applied decorations, 38″ wide, 20″ deep, 61″ high. In Texas, **$1,700.**

Walnut Renaissance Revival dressing case with white marble on two decks and top, molded pediment with applied panels, candle shelves on mirror frame, burl veneer panels on frame and drawers, and ebony and gilt pulls, (teardrops); 51″ wide, 19″ deep, 91″ high. In Texas, **$1,450.**

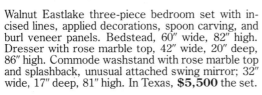

Walnut Eastlake three-piece bedroom set with incised lines, applied decorations, spoon carving, and burl veneer panels. Bedstead, 60″ wide, 82″ high. Dresser with rose marble top, 42″ wide, 20″ deep, 86″ high. Commode washstand with rose marble top and splashback, unusual attached swing mirror; 32″ wide, 17″ deep, 81″ high. In Texas, **$5,500** the set.

Walnut common washstand with spool turned towel bars, 25″ wide, 15″ deep, 29″ high. In Connecticut, **$175.**

Common washstand of mixed woods, with spool turned legs; 26″ wide, 15″ deep, 33″ high. In Pennsylvania, **$155.**

Commode washstand with carved nut pulls on drawer, arched molding on doors, applied design on apron; 32″ wide, 17″ deep, 30″ to top, back rail 5″. In Illinois, **$485.**

Chestnut commode washstand with carved pulls, soap or candle shelves on back rail; 30″ wide, 17″ deep, 30″ to top, back rail 10″. In Illinois, **$395.**

Walnut commode washstand with ebony and gilt pulls (teardrops), raised panels; 30″ wide, 16″ deep, 35″ high. In Illinois, **$400.**

Commode washstand with burl panels, soap or candle shelves on back rail, and applied decorations; 30″ wide, 16″ deep, 36″ high. In Iowa, **$425.**

Walnut commode washstand with white marble top, circular molding on drawer and doors; 31″ wide, 16″ deep, 29″ high. In Pennsylvania, **$400.**

Walnut commode washstand with white marble top, splashback, and soap or candle shelves; burl veneer; applied decorations on chamfered stiles; 31″ high, 19″ deep, 30″ to top, splashback 12″. In Illinois, **$900.** Electrified kerosene lamp, **$225.**

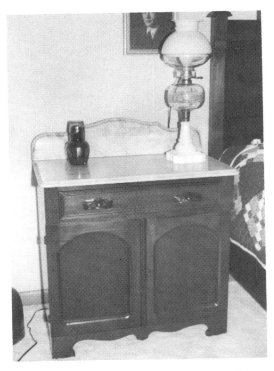

Walnut commode washstand with white marble top and splashback, molded door panels; 30″ wide, 18″ deep, 28″ to top, splashback 7″. In Ohio, **$550.**

Walnut commode washstand with white marble top and splashback, circular molding on drawer, and molded door panels; 30″ wide, 17″ deep, 30″ to top, splashback 8″. In Texas, **$650.**

Walnut Eastlake commode washstand with white marble top, splashback, and soap or candle shelves; burl veneer panels; 30″ wide, 18″ deep, 30″ to top, splashback 12″. In Pennsylvania, **$575.**

Walnut Eastlake commode washstand with brown marble top, incised lines, and spoon carving; 30″ wide, 17″ deep, 27″ high. In Iowa, **$400.**

114

Walnut somnoe with white marble top and splash-back, and circular molding; 19″ high, 17″ deep, 29″ to top, splashback 10″. In Texas, **$550.**

Walnut small bureau washstand with white marble top, 20″ wide, 16″ deep, 35″ high. In Texas, **$800.** Webb Peach Blow vase with blue and gold, **$750.**

Walnut somnoe with white marble top, applied carvings on chamfered stiles, applied panels, and molded door; 20″ wide, 19″ deep, 31″ high. In Texas, **$500.**

Close-up of belt-loop pull on somnoe.

Walnut bureau washstand with block molding on drawers and applied decorations on stiles, 28″ wide, 19″ deep, 34″ high. In Iowa, **$325.**

Walnut somnoe with white marble top and applied carvings on drawer, door, and chamfered stiles; 21″ wide, 20″ deep, 30″ high. In Illinois, **$750.**

Walnut bureau washstand with projection top drawer, applied decorations on chamfered stiles, and circular molding on drawers; 30″ wide, 16″ deep, 30″ high. In Illinois, **$325.**

Walnut bureau washstand with burl panels, 30″ wide, 16″ deep, 30″ high. In Indiana, **$275.** Walnut oval mirror, 18″ wide, 21″ high, **$135.**

Walnut bureau washstand with pilasters, burl veneer, and incised lines; 30″ wide, 17″ deep, 31″ high. In Indiana, **$325.**

Walnut bureau washstand with carved pulls, 29″ wide, 17″ deep, 28″ to top, 4″ back rail. In Ohio, **$325.**

Walnut bureau washstand with raised panels on drawers, 28″ wide, 15″ deep, 28″ high. In Ohio, **$325.**

Walnut bureau washstand with raised panels, retractable towel bar, and soap or candle shelves on splashback; 29″ wide, 17″ deep, 31″ high, 10″ splashback. In Illinois, **$445.**

Walnut bureau washstand with towel bar ends, 31″ wide, 17″ deep, 31″ high. In Iowa, **$325.**

Walnut bureau washstand with carved pulls, 30″ wide, 16″ deep, 29″ high, 9″ splashback. In Wisconsin, **$325.** Brass candleholders, **$135** a pair.

Walnut towel rack, 24″ long, 8″ deep, 31″ high. In Virginia, **$85.**

Walnut quilt rack with Gothic feel, 28″ long, 35″ high. In Illinois, **$225.**

Walnut four-drawer chest with beading on top, applied decorations on chamfered stiles, and convex center on veneered drawers; 42″ wide, 22″ deep, 34″ high. In Alabama, **$475.**

Walnut Eastlake dresser with brown marble top, burl veneer, and incised lines; 44″ wide, 19″ deep, 31″ high. In Maryland, **$550.**

Walnut chest with burl panels, twisted pilasters, and brass pulls; 32″ wide, 22″ deep, 43″ high. In Iowa, **$875.**

Walnut Eastlake dresser with rose marble top, incised lines, and veneer panels; 40″ wide, 17″ deep, 33″ high. In Iowa, **$475.**

Ash dresser with wishbone mirror, 39″ wide, 19″ deep, 73″ high. In Texas, **$600.**

Walnut stained dresser with swing mirror, 41″ wide, 18″ deep, 64″ high. In Iowa, **$525.**

Walnut stained dresser with folk art feel, carved gallery with comb case, two decks with porcelain pulls, raised panels, spoon-carved flowers on drawers, and metal handles; 43″ wide, 20″ deep, 58″ high. In Wisconsin, **$295.**

Walnut Empire transitional dresser with wishbone mirror set in back of lift-lid box, two decks, applied decorations and scroll pilasters on stiles, circular molding on drawers, and projection top and bottom drawers; 40″ wide, 19″ deep, 77″ high. In Iowa, **$850.**

Walnut dresser with two decks, ebony and gilt pulls (teardrops) on molded panels, and applied decorations on chamfered stiles; 41″ wide, 19″ deep, 43″ high. In Illinois, **$595.**

Walnut dresser with white marble insert between two decks, wishbone mirror; 39″ wide, 18″ deep, 69″ high. In Alabama, **$675.**

Walnut dresser with white marble insert between two decks, circular molding on drawers; 40″ wide, 20″ deep, 39″ high. In Alabama, **$425.**

Walnut dresser with crotch mahogany veneer and beading on drawer fronts, applied carved escutcheons, and applied decorations on chamfered stiles; 42″ wide, 19″ deep, 42″ high. In Iowa, **$375.** Separate walnut mirror with applied decorations on molded frame; 24″ wide, 45″ high. **$150.**

Walnut dresser with swing mirror, pediment with missing apex, candle shelves and applied decorations on mirror frame, applied decorations on chamfered stiles, raised panels on drawers, and ebony and gilt pulls (teardrops); 40″ wide, 18″ deep, 81″ high. In Iowa, **$550.**

Walnut veneered serpentine dresser with white marble top, wishbone mirror, and lift-lid box, 42″ wide, 21″ deep, 72″ high. In Alabama, **$595.**

Walnut dresser with attached mirror, candle shelves, two lift-lid boxes, raised panels on drawers, and rounded stiles; 42″ wide, 21″ deep, 79″ high. In Virginia, **$695.**

Walnut dresser with white marble insert between two decks, swing mirror, raised panels on drawers, ebony and gilt pulls, (teardrops); 39″ wide, 17″ deep, 71″ high. In Ohio, **$575.**

Walnut Renaissance Revival dressing case with white marble on two decks and top; molded carved pediment with burled panels, roundels, and candle shelves on mirror frame; burled raised panels on drawers, and ebony and gilt pulls (teardrops); 46″ wide, 18″ deep, 88″ high. In Iowa, **$775.**

Walnut dresser with white marble top, grape and leaf carved pulls, circular molding on drawers with center molded and carved medallions, and pilasters on stiles; 45″ wide, 20″ deep, 32″ high. In Pennsylvania, **$450.**

Walnut Renaissance Revival dressing case with carved pediment and candle shelves on mirror frame, applied burl panels on drawers and frame; 42″ high, 18″ deep, 88″ high. In Iowa, **$450.**

Ebonized walnut Renaissance Revival dressing case with white marble tops, molded pediment with scrolls and candle shelves on mirror frame; 63″ wide, 19″ deep, 94″ high. In Illinois, **$2,075.**

Walnut and rosewood Renaissance Revival dressing case with white marble tops, molded and paneled pediment, roundels, and veneered panels; 17″ wide, 19″ deep, 98″ high. In Illinois, **$2,985.**

Walnut Renaissance Revival, Eastlake influence dressing case with brown marble tops, roundels, chip carving, and burl veneer panels; 58″ wide, 20″ deep, 95″ high. In Maryland, **$950.**

Walnut rococo dresser, with white marble top, swing mirror with fretwork, candle shelves, two small mirrors, and circular molding on veneered drawers; 45″ wide, 23″ deep, 84″ high. In Texas, **$1,300.**

Walnut Eastlake dresser with brown marble top, burl veneer on cylinder under mirror, and incised lines; 46″ wide, 22″ deep, 85″ high. In Texas, **$1,750.**

Walnut rococo étagère dresser with white marble top, two lift-lid boxes, fretwork mirror frame with shelves, carved crest, applied decorations on stiles, burl veneer panels on drawers, and slipper drawer (secret drawer) in apron; 53″ wide, 25″ deep, 86″ high. In Texas, **$1,750.**

Walnut dresser with white marble top, veneered wishbone mirror frame, lift-lid box, veneered drawers, veneer panels, and applied decorations on chamfered stiles; 42″ wide, 24″ deep, 79″ high. In Alabama, **$795.**

Walnut dresser with white marble top, applied decorations and candle shelves on swing mirror frame,
two lift-lid boxes, swell front, circular molding
on veneered drawers, and applied decorations on
chamfered stiles; 43″ wide, 20″ deep, 80″ high. In
Illinois, **$1,395.**

Walnut Renaissance Revival dresser, Eastlake influence with white marble top, incised pediment, pilasters, shelves, and applied roundels, 46″ wide, 18″
deep, 92″ high. In Alabama, **$850.**

Walnut chiffonier (also called sidelock) with hinged
stile locks, burl veneer panels, and small drawer
on top; 40″ wide, 19″ deep, 68″ high. In Illinois,
$1,685.

Walnut Eastlake chiffonier (also called sidelock) with
hinged stile locks, burl veneer panels, and incised
lines; 37″ wide, 19″ deep, 62″ high. In Iowa, **$1,050.**

Walnut Eastlake chiffonier (also called sidelock), attached mirror with two parallel drawers, burl veneer panels, and incised lines; 34″ wide, 18″ deep, 72″ high. In Illinois, **$950.**

Walnut bedstead with carved pediment, urn finials, and applied decorations; 56″ wide, 76″ long, 65″ high. In Ohio, **$575.** Quilt, **$250.**

Walnut rococo bedstead with carved pediment and applied decorations, 53″ wide, 57″ high headboard, 35″ high footboard. In Iowa, **$350.**

Walnut bedstead with molded and paneled pediment, molded panels on head and footboards; 62″ wide, 89″ high. In Texas, **$2,200.**

Walnut Renaissance Revival, Eastlake influence bedstead with molded pediment, burl veneer panels, and incised lines; 55″ wide, 73″ high. In Iowa, **$650.**

Walnut bedstead with ebony and gilt decorations, eclectic (Rococo, Renaissance Revival and Eastlake), style, urn finials, bronze medallion, burl veneer panels, and applied decorations; 51″ wide, 82″ high. In Arkansas, **$2,000.**

Close-up of medallion on walnut bedstead.

Walnut Renaissance Revival bedstead with burl veneer panels, molded pediment, and applied decorations; 54″ wide, 67″ high. In Iowa, **$750.**

Walnut Eastlake bedstead with burl veneer panels, spoon carving, incised lines, and applied roundels; 58″ wide, 83″ high. In Alabama, **$850.**

Walnut tester bedstead with turned posts, 58″ wide, 84″ high. In Texas, **$1,400.**

Rosewood dressing table with white marble top, molded pediment, candle shelves, X-shaped stretcher, and cabriole legs; 46″ wide, 22″ deep, 72″ high. In Missouri, **$1,200.**

Walnut rococo two-piece bedroom set. Bedstead with molded pediment, applied decorations, and circular molding; 57″ wide, 78″ high. Dresser with white marble top, lift-lid boxes, applied decorations, and circular molding on drawers; 31″ wide, 18″ deep, 80″ high. In Pennsylvania, **$1,350** the set.

Walnut Eastlake three-piece bedroom set with incised lines and burl veneer panels. Bedstead, 74″ high. Dresser with white marble top and swing mirror; 39″ wide, 19″ deep, 77″ high. Commode washstand with white marble top, splashback with soap or candle shelves; 29″ wide, 16″ deep, 39″ high. In Texas, **$2,495** the set.

Walnut Renaissance Revival two-piece bedroom set. Bedstead with applied roundels, burl veneer panels, and molded pediment; 61″ wide, 105″ high. Dressing case with marble tops, burl veneer panels, applied roundels, molded pediment, ebony and gilt pulls (teardrops), and slipper drawer (secret drawer) in apron; 48″ wide, 22″ deep, 98″ high. In Texas, **$8,500** the set.

Walnut shaving stand with white marble top, swing mirror that can be raised and lowered, and pedestal base; 16″ wide, 16″ deep, 68″ high. In Texas, **$600.**

Walnut Renaissance Revival two-piece bedroom set. Bedstead with molded pediment, urn finials, applied roundels, and burl veneer panels; 57″ wide, 87″ high. Dressing case with white marble tops, molded pediment, applied roundels, burl veneer panels, candle shelves, and ebony and gilt pulls (teardrops); 46″ wide, 20″ deep, 84″ high. In Missouri, **$2,750** the set.

Walnut wardrobe with applied fruit carvings, circular molding; 42″ high, 19″ deep, 87″ high. From the home of Mark Hanna, a businessman and politician who helped William McKinley be elected president in 1896. In Indiana, **$1,250.**

Walnut Eastlake two-piece bedroom set. Bedstead with incised lines, applied roundels, and burl veneer panels; 58″ wide, 82″ long. Dresser with white marble top, incised lines, applied roundels, and burl veneer panels; 43″ wide, 19″ deep, 81″ high. In Iowa, **$1,950** the set.

Walnut wardrobe (sometimes called armoire) with burl veneer panels, cornice top, and knock-down construction for ease in transporting; 51″ wide, 17″ deep, 82″ high. In Texas, **$1,000.**

Mahogany wardrobe (sometimes called armoire) with cornice top, applied decorations, pilasters, and knock-down construction for ease in transporting; 36″ wide, 19″ deep, 89″ high. In Virginia, **$925.**

Walnut wardrobe (sometimes called armoire) with arched molding on doors, and beading on apron. In Iowa, **$850.**

Walnut Renaissance Revival, Eastlake influence wardrobe (sometimes called armoire) with spoon carving, burl veneer panels, incised lines, and molded pediment; 52″ wide, 20″ deep, 105″ high. In Iowa, **$1,275.**

8

Nursery Needs

A man once asked the mother of a wee baby why she closed drawers and doors with a push of her feet, knees, or derrière. The answer was simple. When the hands are full, other parts are assigned additional tasks. Victorian parents knew this. Why should a woman be idle as she rocked the baby in a cradle? If she could step up and down on a foot pedal to keep the infant swaying, she could simultaneously operate a butter churn.

Cradles in the 1700s were enclosed as much as possible to help keep drafts off the infants. They had solid sides and hoods and usually were crafted from pine from the nearby forests.

By the 1800s, when stoves helped heat homes better, the baby's bed could be more open. Walnut, rather than pine, was frequently selected for its construction. Spindles, some plain and some turned, replaced the solid sides. Turnings that resembled a series of balls rather than a string of spools were featured on many cribs. Articles with this construction were referred to as spool furniture. While some cradles of the late 1800s still rocked, many were suspended from frames and swung instead. Patents were issued, and often a locking device

was incorporated so that the cradle's movement could be restrained. As a consequence, the child was protected from a possible fall.

It would be difficult to peer up at adult furniture all the time. Occasionally, pint-sized furniture was created especially for children so that they could look in a mirror at their level or recline on a chaise longue that was just their size. The designs emulated adult furnishings. Because these items are unusual and collectors enjoy them, small models bring good prices.

What child doesn't enjoy the motion of a rocking chair? Small versions of rockers followed popular styles. Since caning was farmed out by the factories, the wives of workers often hand-caned chairs, and the older children often assisted them. A horse-drawn wagon distributed and picked up the work.

Patent furniture pleased the people in the latter half of the nineteenth century. A highchair with several positions was popular then. Its popularity continues, and today many doll collectors like such petite furniture so that they can display "babies" from their collections. Occasionally, highchairs functioned as both a place for feeding and as a go-cart. Neither babies nor children were neglected by furniture designers during the Victorian Era.

Walnut cradle swings on frame with lock hook and pedal for swinging, 42″ wide, 21½″ deep, 35½″ high. In Texas, **$850.**

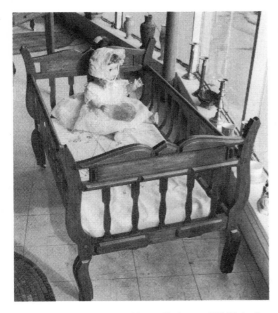

Walnut baby bed, 42″ wide, 27″ deep, 28″ high. In Illinois, **$350.**

Walnut cradle on frame, 38″ wide, 20½″ deep, 36″ high. In Illinois, **$735.**

Walnut and maple youth bed, 65″ long, 40½″ wide, 49½″ high. In South Carolina, **$395.**

Butternut-stained walnut child's doll dresser with ebony and gilt pulls (teardrops), 17½″ wide, 9½″ deep, 36½″ high. In Iowa, **$295.**

Child's walnut cane-bottom chair with chip carving and burl panels, 18″ arm to arm, 29″ high. In Illinois, **$210.**

Child's walnut dresser with molded and paneled pediment, white marble top, two decks (handkerchief boxes), burl panels, chamfered stiles, and slipper drawer (secret drawer) in apron; 36″ wide, 21½″ deep, 76½″ high. In Texas, **$1,250.**

Child's walnut chest of drawers with burl panels, 29″ wide, 18½″ deep, 32½″ high, in Illinois, **$495.**

Child's patented highchair in upright position, 35½″ high.

Child's chaise longue (fainting couch), 39″ wide, 12″ deep, 15½″ high. In Pennsylvania, **$150.**

Child's walnut highchair in go-cart position, 40″ long base, 27½″ high to top of handle. In Texas, **$600.**

9

Big Names in Nineteenth-Century Furniture

Blow the bugles! Clang the cymbals! Roll the drums! Here are some of the Big Names in the nineteenth-century furniture-making industry.

Joseph Meeks was first listed as a New York cabinetmaker in the 1798 city directory. He was later joined by his sons, and they produced furniture that kept abreast of the fashions of the times during the seventy years they were in business. John Belter, with his elaborate, decorative, carved and pierced rococo with naturalistic motifs, is perhaps the best known of the Victorian furniture makers. Among his contemporaries was Charles A. Baudouine, who crafted quality products.

A creative furniture designer from New Orleans was Prudent Mallard, whose half tester beds included a special frame for mosquito netting that extended down from the canopy to protect southern sleepers from these buzzing, biting insects. John Jelliff of Newark, New Jersey, liked to carve warriors and women with long flowing tresses. He frequently used them as arm supports on chairs with the Renaissance Revival styling. There were many fine furniture factories in other locales as well. Grand Rapids, Michigan, with its nearby forests, contributed generously to the industry and has been referred to as the era's furniture capital. On the Ohio River, Cincinnati shipped its products easily to many areas. It would be difficult to incorporate all the industry's Big Names, but the works of the ones selected indicate some of the changing fashions that prevailed during the Victorian period.

Most homes included furniture that was not purchased at one time from a single source. For example, as shown in the photograph, a duet of rococo Rosalie side chairs, circa late 1850s, might flank an oval marble-top table with a carved apron, pendant finials, and an ornate pedestal base. The Eastlake mirror with pilasters and incised lines dates to the late 1800s, and the painted electric lamp has a 1920s look. The photograph shows that it is possible to unite pieces from various time periods to form an interesting whole.

Joseph Meeks and Sons was a cabinetmaking family that worked from 1798 to 1868. While it was not the practice to buy suites of furniture as such in 1833, purchasers could coordinate their bedchambers by selecting similar styles and sizes of furniture from the Meeks establishment. The full-length, swinging, cheval mirror was introduced (see Chapter Seven), and the new gondola chair could serve in the dining room or as a side chair in the parlor (see Chapter Three). When a new fashion was favored, the Meeks family followed the prevailing fad and shipped their products all over the nation. Their showrooms in New Orleans promoted sales and helped rate

Pair of Belter rosewood Rosalie side chairs, 36" high. **$2,500** apiece. Walnut center table with white marble top, pendant finials, molded apron, and pedestal base; 30" wide, 22" deep, 30" high. In Illinois, **$850.**

Walnut Eastlake mirror with pilasters and incised lines, 23" wide, 51" high. In Illinois, **$150.**

them among the leading New York City furniture makers. Maybe Washington, D.C., diplomats sat on Meeks Gothic revival chairs — a sales bill shows that some were purchased for the White House in 1846 and 1847 during James K. Polk's presidency. When the rococo ornamentations from the past were resurrected, the Meeks family manufactured this style too. Some of the Meeks works seem to imitate John Belter's examples.

John Belter (1795-1863) immigrated to the United States from Germany. He was partial to rosewood, which came from Brazil and India and was named for its rose scent. From the wood, Belter carved roses and leaves and pierced the surface to create ornamental naturalistic designs. He bent chair backs into shapes that pleased the eye and body but were treacherous to the wood, since solid woods tend to split along the grain when they are mistreated. This problem only tantalized John Belter. He knew that men in the past had achieved a strong base for working with wood by laminating it. In this process, layers of wood are glued together so that the grains of successive pieces are at right angles to each other. For example, on one layer, the grain is placed horizontally, followed by a vertical strip. This pattern is followed until the desired thickness is achieved. The average number of thin layers of rosewood ranged from six to eight, but in some instances it could be half or twice that depending upon the work that was to be done. Then Belter used steam and a special matrix to curve the wood into the shape he desired. His furniture was ornate and constructed with precision. Students of rococo furniture usually award it the gold medal because his craftsmanship was synonymous with quality and beauty. See the Color Section for Belter furniture.

Have you ever visited the Rosalie mansion at Natchez, Mississippi? A pattern known to be associated with John Belter is on display there. The story goes that the daughter of this stately home's owners studied in New York City in about 1859 or 1860, just prior to the Civil War. She supposedly purchased parlor furniture from John Belter for her parents' home. Her selection became known as Rosalie, and with slight variations, is the most common surviving example of parlor seating associated with Belter. The design could be purchased with or

Close-up of Belter rosewood Rosalie chair with rose and grape carving on crest and roses on legs and apron.

Back of Belter rosewood Rosalie side chair showing typical bent back and leg construction.

without clusters of hanging grapes, with minor changes in the shape of the seat, or with the carvings (not piercings) varying slightly in detail and arrangement. A photograph showing the back and front of a rosewood Rosalie chair can be seen in this chapter.

To collectors, Belter's ornamentations were distinctive and imaginative, yet realistic. A rose might be depicted as a bud, before it reached full bloom, or it might be mature and completely opened. By comparison, the works of other designers appeared to have less depth, less realism, and less grace, as if they copied nature from a carefully followed diagram. While his contemporaries created various styles from Gothic to Renaissance Revival, Belter apparently preferred and steadfastly remained true to the rococo influence.

The solid carved Rosalie meridienne shown is really a petite chaise longue made from rosewood. Left- and right-sided versions were available. The brocatelle (brocatel), an upholstery material that usually combined silk and linen, has figures similar to those on brocade. Among the Abraham and Mary Todd Lincoln's furnishings in their Springfield, Illinois, home was a pierced-carved Belter meridienne that Mrs. Lincoln sold following her husband's death. Now it resides in the Henry Ford Museum at Dearborn, Michigan.

It is important to realize that John Belter did not always select rosewood, but his most handsome pieces seem to have been made from this wood. Mahogany, stained oak, and blackwood (hardwood painted to emulate ebony) could be relatively simple in their design or ornate when Belter used them. Usually leaves and flowers were intertwined as connecting sweeps between pierced-carved motifs. Generally, his peers depended on C scrolls as linking mechanisms. Pierced carving was not always employed, and chair backs did not have to be constructed out of spherical, cylindrical, or conical molded shapes that looked as if the entire back was one piece. This master craftsman did not work only with laminated woods, but could carve from solid blocks also, and sometimes he applied carvings. For instance, the cresting on a chair might be added to the back frame. Some feel that Belter did not seam veneer, but think that his laminated chair backs rolled around in one continuous piece. In reality,

Belter rosewood left-sided Rosalie meridienne, or recamier, with rose and grape carving on crest rail and button-tufted back, 40″ wide. In Illinois, **$8,300.**

they were seamed with such care and deliberation that the seams are invisible.

Another example of carving from nature's models is shown on the crest of a Belter work that is now called a Henry Clay chair. Statesman Henry Clay (1777-1852), the noted orating senator who served during the stressful time prior to the Civil War, was disappointed that he was not elected president of the United States. As he worked to preserve the Union, he declared, "I'd rather be right than president." His showplace home, Ashland, was located outside of Lexington, Kentucky, and he bought exquisite furnishings for it, including some from John Belter's company. Belter established his New York shop in 1844, just eight years prior to Mr. Clay's demise. A photograph shows a close-up of the solid carving on the crest of a Henry Clay chair that is flanked by two Rosalie chairs.

Little of Belter's parlor furniture had plain molded legs. Most examples feature elegant carving, often with a floral motif. The cabriole type that bulged at the knee, swept in to the ankle, then out a little to form a double curve, was Frenchlike in appearance. The front of the back legs on chairs may be rounded, but the back is generally flat. On many Victorian pieces designed for sitting, casters appear only on the front legs. Mr. Belter liked to put rollers, preferably of brass, on all four legs. While he apparently produced more parlor furniture than any other type, he did make some furnishings for the dining room and the bedchamber.

For the true student of John Belter's work there is a book that explains the results of scientific studies of laminated furniture. The in-depth examination included X-rays and exacting measurements. *The Furniture of John Henry Belter and the Rococo Revival* by Marvin D. Schwartz, Edward J. Stanek, and Douglas K. True was published in 1981 by E. P. Dutton, New York. It shows how much the authors appreciate the artistry of this craftsman.

Three Belter rosewood chairs. The center chair is in the Henry Clay pattern, and the two outer ones are Rosalie; all 36″ high. In Arkansas, **$2,000** each.

Close-up of crest on Belter rosewood Henry Clay chair showing detailed carving.

Close-up of crest on Belter rosewood Rosalie chair showing the detailed carving.

Three rosewood rococo pieces from a five-piece parlor set in the Belter style with Meek characteristics, showing C scrolls, rose carved crest, and pierced carving. Sofa, 56″ arm to arm, 47″ high. Armchair, 24″ arm to arm, 44″ high. Side chair, 41″ high. In Arkansas, **$10,000** for the five-piece set.

144

The name of cabinetmaker Charles A. Baudouine appeared in the New York directory from the 1830s to the mid-1850s. He took frequent voyages to his homeland, France, and was cognizant of styles that prevailed there. A former employee wrote that his company, with its nearly two hundred workers, produced rosewood "parlour suits" with round perforated backs as well as matching marble-top side and center tables and elaborate étagères. Because of his statements, some unmarked quality rococo furniture that has the Belter feel has been associated with Baudouine. His known works show skilled craftsmanship but are not laminated. A fire screen that is reminiscent of both Charles Baudouine's and Prudent Mallard's techniques appears in the Color Section.

An elite étagère in the Color Section exhibits Mallard qualities. A rosewood dressing table with a black marble top accentuated with gold veins is done in the Mallard manner, too. Caryatids (female figures that serve as supporting columns) hold the swinging mirror. Their hair is short, and their eyes are different on each pillar — a characteristic that helps identify this man's work. Prudent Mallard's furniture represented expansive, expensive splendor. It seemed as at home in the spacious antebellum southern mansions as the heavy walnut church pump organs apparently felt in their ecclesiastical settings. Furniture pieces attributed to Prudent Mallard are generally the only examples of nineteenth-century efforts that rank with Belter's for their gracefully carved ornamentations and desirable workmanship. Rosewood and marble were Prudent's favorites, although he utilized mahogany and oak as well. He also imported French furnishings and favored rococo and Renaissance styles. Mallard was born in 1809 in France of a French mother and a Scottish father. He was twenty years old when he immigrated to the United States, finally settling in New Orleans, Louisiana, where he died in 1879.

John Jelliff began working in Newark, New Jersey, in 1835. He designed Gothic furniture

Rosewood dressing table in the style of Prudent Mallard, with black marble top that has "gold" veins, caryatids (female figures as supporting columns), swinging mirror, rope legs, and beading; 42″ wide, 21″ deep, 66″ high. In Arkansas, **$2,500.** Bradley and Hubbard kerosene lamp (not electrified), 18″ high. **$400.**

Close-up of caryatid (female figure used as supporting column) on dressing table made in the Prudent Mallard style, 24″ high.

with cutout arched patterns, and he created rococo works. When rococo curves, flowers, fruits, nuts, and leaves went out of style, Jelliff turned to Renaissance Revival interpretations. Fashion demanded a bulkier, rectangular look with some leg features and appendages borrowed from Louis XVI styles. Jelliff obliged, usually selecting walnut and rosewood for his work. From solid woods he carved caryatids (females) and atlantes (their male counterparts), both of which formed supporting columns, to hold up the arms of sofas and chairs. He liked his walnut women to have long, flowing hair and men to show macho, warrior images. Other designers presented similar styles, but now many pieces with comparable characteristics are attributed to Jelliff, "made in the Jelliff manner," or described as resembling his work, though they have not been documented. His quality workmanship is appreciated by those who find Renaissance lines aesthetically pleasing. He died in 1893.

As the Victorian period ended, Charles Lock(e) Eastlake (1836-1906) led a revolt against fancy, fussy furniture. He felt boxy lines conserved wood and were stronger than curves. His works were described as "Eastlake." Examples of such pieces can be found by referring to the Index.

Rosewood side chair from three-piece Jelliff Renaissance Revival set, with female warrior in back metal medallion; 40″ high.

Close-up of metal medallion with female warrior and crest from Jelliff side chair.

Rosewood gentleman's chair from three-piece Jelliff Renaissance Revival set, with male warrior head in back medallion, atlantes arms; 28″ arm to arm, 42″ high. In Texas, **$5,000,** the set, including sofa shown in the Color section.

Close-up of atlantes (male figure used as supporting column) on Jelliff armchair, 8″ high.

Close-up of metal medallion with male warrior and crest of Jelliff gentleman's chair.

Rosewood two-piece Renaissance Revival bedroom set in the Jelliff style. Bedstead with molded pediment, carved female head, burl veneer panels, and applied decorations; 62″ wide, 88″ high. Dressing case (étagère dresser) with white marble tops, molded pediment with carved female head, burl veneer panels, molded drawers, and applied decorations; 55″ wide, 22″ deep, 93″ high. In Arkansas, **$7,500** the set. Seth Thomas clock, marbleized over wood; 17″ wide, 7″ deep, 11″ high, **$300.**

Top shelves: Wave Crest box on left, 4″ diameter, 3″ high. Wave Crest box on right, 3″ square, 3″ high. **$250** each. Bottom shelves: Left, Kelba vase of opaque glass with pink floral enamel design. **$350.** Right, blue diamond-quilted ewer, 8″ high. **$300.** Biscuit jars on marble tops: Left, 6″ diameter, 9″ high. Right, 5″ square, 7″ high. **$250** each.

Close-up of head on rosewood étagère dresser possibly made by Jelliff.

Walnut Jelliff armchair with molded crest, burl medallion, caryatid support arms, applied decorations, and burl veneer panels; 28" arm to arm, 45" high. In Arkansas, **$800.**

Close-up of caryatid (female figure used as supporting column) on Jelliff armchair, 9" high.

10

Enchanting Accessories

How could a delicate Victorian young woman play a pump organ? It required athletic power and coordination to pump with the feet, push with the knees, pull out stops, and glide the hands over the keyboard. If she made a few mistakes, who cared? It was fun to gather around the organ and harmonize on a Sunday afternoon. In the evening, flickering oil-burning lamps could be placed on the stands provided for that purpose, and both the player and the singers could share the sheet music. Of course, some type of seat was required by the organist. An unusual one that shows the Eastlake lines of the late 1870s has knobs at the ends. By turning these in the proper direction, it is possible to adjust the height, raising or lowering the stool as required. This uncommon walnut bench has rounded legs that assume an X shape, a style that can be traced back to Roman times. They are referred to as curule legs.

Other small stools had specific functions. Those known today as footstools were called footrests in the 1800s. One type of small bench was higher, and the top was hinged to lift up. Since slippers could be kept inside, this piece of furniture was advertised as a footrest frame with slipper box. Now it is generally termed a slipper bench. Ladies of the past liked to create needlepoint to upholster the top, and women today use their skills with needles and woolen threads to fashion designs on fabric, too.

It is common for objects to appear in homes today that would not have been acceptable years ago. Who would want a dental cabinet in the parlor, even when it was fancy enough to resemble a desk? The current trend of adopting professional and store pieces from the past probably would be laughable to their original owners, yet some of those pieces are attractive as well as practical. Many had a series of small

Walnut organ with fretwork and stick construction, made by Estey Organ Company, Brattleboro, Vermont; 44″ wide, 22″ deep, 71″ high. In Texas, **$1,350.**

Walnut piano bench that can be raised and lowered by screwing knobs on each end, curule legs, incised lines, and applied roundels; 20″ wide, 15″ deep, 19″ high. In Arkansas, **$600.**

drawers, which are useful for storage. Jewelry, scarves, and collections of fishing lures or pocket knives are just a few of the items now filling old spool cabinets. Such creative touches personalize a home.

Mirrors not only are useful, they can be decorative as well. The easel type, which stood on top of chests of drawers, tables, or washstands, could be elaborate in appearance. Collectors familiar with names appreciate the decorative metal frames that were produced by the firm of Bradley and Hubbard Manufacturing Company, Meriden, Connecticut, in the early 1900s. Their stock included metal boxes, candlesticks, dippers, coal hods, desk sets, bookends, and quality lamps. Their logo incorporated two triangles, one inside the other, framing the company's name. In the center of the smaller triangle was an Aladdin's lamp similar to the one from which the fabled genie escaped.

Special hat racks hung on walls in Victorian homes. On some, a woman again could illustrate her deftness with a needle. She might copy Berlin work with strands of worsted wool to achieve patterns similar to those that the Germans created and named for their leading city. Frames with hooks or bars to hold towels also could frame needlepoint pictures. Many ladies seemed to enjoy creative craft projects.

Comb cases abounded when bathrooms were not a part of the home and grooming was done over a basin in the kitchen or in the bedroom. Men and women needed a handy place to keep combs or a shaving brush and razor. If a mirror or a bar to hold a towel was included, the utility of the case increased. A wooden wall pocket was a handy place to put the newspaper or a current issue of a magazine. A fabric type, wider at the top and narrower at the base, was called a slipper pocket. Shelves for the bric-a-brac that the Victorian housewife seemed to crave came in all sizes and shapes. Of course, clock shelves were popular, too.

Walnut slipper bench with lift lid and raised veneer panels, 20″ wide, 11″ deep, 18″ high. In Illinois, **$200.**

Walnut dental cabinet with white marble top, burl panels, and pull-out writing shelf; 33″ wide, 21″ deep, 69″ high. In Illinois, **$2,850.**

Brass easel mirror made by Bradley and Hubbard, 12″ high. In Alabama, **$195.**

Inside view of dental cabinet.

Walnut hat rack with Berlin-work insert, 21″ wide, 11″ high. In Illinois, **$135.**

Walnut comb case with lift lid box beneath mirror, 12″ wide, 4″ deep, 24″ high. In Illinois, **$110.**

Walnut comb case with incised lines, 17″ wide, 3″ deep, 23″ high. In Ohio, **$145.**

Walnut wall pocket with carved Columbia head, 16" wide, 23" high. In Missouri, **$200**.

Walnut slipper wall pocket with Berlin work, 14" wide, 4" deep, 28" high. In Illinois, **$275**.

Decorative frames were common. Sometimes the pane of glass, either front or back, was painted. When the decoration was on the back, it was referred to as a reverse painting, since the design had to be put on backwards. This took skill, and the artist had to constantly check the front to be sure that the work was coming out as desired.

Shadow boxes were popular Victorian decorations. They were made of a deep frame into which a three-dimensional arrangement could be placed. Dried flowers, feathers, or hair often were used. *Godey's Magazine and Lady's Book* influenced trends and included instructions for craft projects. When women brushed their long locks, they rolled up the hair that came off the brush and poked it into a small round bowl that had a lift lid with a hole in the middle. *Godey's* provided information on how to twist or form the strands into watch chains, bracelets, brooches, or pictures. Because people didn't have pictures to remember their loved ones by,

locks of hair served as a memorial instead. Hair pictures and jewelry from the last half of the 1800s are sought today.

Double frames were common, and some people now separate them to form individual ones. Some had inner or outer liners of gold or wood, or an enamel liner. A composition of plaster at times was built up in molded designs and gilded. When the proper tone was achieved by actually applying sheets of extremely thin pressed gold, the result was known as gold leaf. These strips were laid over an adhesive base on the frame. Evenly spaced lines that correspond to the size of the applied sheets help identify frames gilded by this expensive and time-consuming process.

It is claimed that the first plastic products manufactured in the United States were made of gutta-percha. The product, made from gutta-percha trees that grow in Southeast Asia, was used to make cases for daguerreotypes. A patent for the boxes was issued in 1854, and the boxlike frames were made until around 1880.

Multilinear enamel frame, white alternating with gold; 27″ wide, 31″ high. In Arkansas, **$100.**

Walnut crisscross picture frames with leaves and porcelain tips at corners, 15″ wide, 16″ high. **$185** the pair.

Other types of boxes, album covers, and wall frames were fashioned from this material, too.

Many crisscross frames survived from the Victorian era. They usually had a carved leaf or a porcelain button at each corner.

Lamps were another essential accessory item. A banquet type customarily was tall, with a fancy metal base and a round globe. Brass, bronze or, less commonly, pewter, with filigree work and figures, added exotic touches to these lighting devices. Organ or piano lamps could be raised or lowered as desired. Various oil-burning versions were patented in the late 1800s. Lamps that were suspended from the ceiling sent their glow afar, especially when glass prisms attached to the shade caught the light and added a sparkle to the room. A smoke bell swung above the chimney and helped keep the smoke from the burning fluid from making a dark outline on the ceiling.

In the 1890s, there was an artistic rebellion in Europe and the United States. The French called the new art forms Art Nouveau. Sensu-ous, flowing lines were prominent. The youthful female form was graceful, often depicted with softly draped garments and long tresses. Some were scantily clad or not clothed at all. Floral subjects curved gracefully, and insects were incorporated into designs. This art form was chic until about the 1920s and has experienced a revival. The lamp pictured from this era includes both gas jets and electrical wiring. That's like getting two lamps for the price of one.

Gutta-percha frame, 14″ wide, 15″ high. In Illinois, **$125.**

Hanging lamp with Mt. Washington glass font and shade, crystal prisms, and two amethyst jewels in brass fittings; all original, including smoke bell. In Arkansas, **$1,200.**

Walnut shadow box with hair wreath and gold leaves, 25″ square, 5″ deep. In Illinois, **$200.**

Walnut parlor table with oval gray marble top, burl applied panels on apron and legs, incised lines and applied roundels; 29″ wide, 21″ deep, 28″ high. In Texas, **$750.** Pewter dancing girls banquet lamp with cherub shade, 45″ high. In Texas, **$600.**

Close-up of dancing girls on pewter banquet lamp.

Of course, candles have been used continuously for centuries. Fancy holders usually came in pairs or in threes, with the center one the most exotic of the trio. Called girandoles, these frequently held the place of honor on the mantle. Some had marble bases and were decorated with prisms. One even had a matching metal clock as the functional yet ornamental focal point. All these pieces are metallic.

Connecticut often was called the clock state because of the many clockmakers who congregated there in the days when the United States was a struggling infant nation. In fact, the son of Eli Terry, the man who introduced mass production to the clock industry in this nation, had a town renamed in his honor; in 1831, Terrysville, Connecticut was founded. Eli's new machines to stamp out identical, interchangeable parts and his assembly-line methods replaced the tedious work of making

one clock at a time. As a result, most homeowners could afford clocks.

Seth Thomas, one of Terry's employees, later started his own factory at Plymouth Hollow, a community that became Thomaston in 1866 after the clocks became well known. Elias Ingraham (1805-1885) worked in Bristol, as did Elisha N. Welch (1809-1887). The Gilbert Clock Company was at Winsted. The clocks often incorporated patriotic symbols such as the Statue of Liberty or the head of Columbia, a female figure named by the Negro slave poet Phillis Wheatley. A long case clock, now frequently termed a grandfather clock, was awarded to a commissioner of the World's Columbian Exposition. That celebration was held in 1893 (a year late) to commemorate the landing of Christopher Columbus in the New World in 1492. It was made by J. Smith & Sons of London, England. (See page 175.)

Since clutter was popular in Victorian homes, statues for stands sold well. From about 1859 to 1892, John Rogers made plaster statuary that showed common events of the times, with the titles incised on the edge of the base along with his name. How could people resist such homey themes as the shy young man holding his bashful bride-to-be by the hand, depicted on the statue "Coming to the Parson"? The Slave Mart (later called the Slave Auction), The Checker Players, Weighing the Baby, Playing Doctor, Going for the Cows, Chess, The School Examination, and School Days were subjects with which everyone could identify and enjoy. The backs were as detailed as the fronts, and since they were cast in molds, they were produced in volume. Rogers did mold a few of his groupings from Parian, a marblelike, unglazed ware that at times was tinted blue, rose, or green.

The ornate carvings on Victorian furniture were inspired by flowers, fowl, animals, and people depicted. At times metal plaques, including those of inexpensive pot metal, were utilized.

The Victorian age faded out as Queen Victoria's long life and reign ended in 1901. During her reign, furniture makers experimented with many styles. In spite of their differences, they all are considered Victorian furniture. Extravagant home furnishings of the 1800s gave way to the plainer pieces of the twentieth century. Because walnut trees were becoming scarce, the dark woods gave way to light oak, which began to dominate in the late 1800s and early 1900s. In this manner, an era ended.

Art Nouveau gas and electric bronze table lamp with a feminine configuration, floral lights with glass and bead petals; 33" high. In Illinois, **$2,800.**

Onyx and brass piano lamp that can be raised and lowered, with floral globe, and holder for sheet music. In Texas, **$1,250.**

Close-up of font of onyx and brass piano lamp.

Walnut footstool with cabriole legs, 16″ square, 15″ high. In Pennsylvania, **$155.**

Walnut slipper bench with incised lines, burl panels, and lift lid; 21″ wide, 11″ deep, 17″ high. In Iowa, **$275.**

Walnut slipper bench with burl veneer panels and lift lid, 22″ wide, 11″ deep, 18″ high. In Illinois, **$250.**

Walnut slipper bench, with incised lines and lift lid, 22″ wide, 12″ deep, 20″ high. In Texas, **$300.**

Plated iron easel mirror with swing-out filigree gate, 12″ wide, 12″ high. In Wisconsin, **$95.**

Walnut spool cabinet with thirty drawers, burl veneer panels, and incised lines; 33″ wide, 16″ deep, 45″ high. In Illinois, **$1,295.**

Brass easel mirror made by Bradley and Hubbard, 12″ high. In Alabama, **$125.**

Gold leaf mirror, 31″ wide, 51″ high. In Pennsylvania, **$150.**

161

Walnut mirror with leaf garlands, carved from one piece of wood; 16″ wide, 31″ high. In Illinois, **$425.**

Adjustable walnut hat rack with mirror and porcelain tips on hangers, 24″ wide, 28″ high. In Pennsylvania, **$125.**

Walnut hat rack with needlepoint insert, 21″ wide, 11″ high. In Illinois, **$135.**

162

Walnut towel rack with head crest, incised lines, and needlepoint insert. In Illinois, **$150.**

Walnut comb case with drawer beneath mirror, 12″ wide, 6″ deep, 28″ high. In Iowa, **$97.**

Walnut comb case with cut-work design, 10″ wide, 2″ deep, 14″ high. In Iowa, **$65.**

Walnut and pine comb case with applied hearts, 10″ wide, 3″ deep, 9″ high. In Iowa, **$50.**

Walnut comb case with hairpin holders, 19″ wide, 3″ deep, 17″ high. In Iowa, **$75.**

Walnut wall pocket with flower and leaf carvings, 19″ wide, 22″ high. In Illinois, **$225.**

Walnut folding wall pocket, incised lines, and cherub head that was applied later; 15″ wide, 7″ deep, 19″ high. In Illinois, **$125.**

Walnut double wall pocket with ebonized designs, incised lines; 16″ wide, 7″ deep, 34″ high. In Wisconsin, **$125.**

Dark-stained lattice wall rack, 12″ wide, 4″ deep, 13″ high. In Iowa, **$52.**

Walnut crisscross frame with applied leaves at corners, 9″ wide, 11″ high. In Iowa, **$35.** Shelf, stained dark; 10″ wide, 5″ deep, 13″ high, **$40.**

Walnut folding shelf with carved bird and leaves, 9″ wide, 5″ deep, 11″ high. In Iowa, **$80.**

Walnut shelf with incised lines and drawer, 24″ wide, 7″ deep, 7″ high. In Ohio, **$125.** Clear glass chamber lamp, **$70.**

Walnut shelf, 8″ wide, 4″ deep, 7″ high. In Iowa, **$65.**

166

Walnut shelf with open work, 11″ wide, 5″ deep, 21″ high. In Iowa, **$65.**

Walnut wall shelf with carved cherub head, 14″ wide, 9″ deep, 18″ high. In Iowa, **$225.**

Walnut shelf with incised lines, 12″ wide, 6″ deep, 12″ high. In Iowa, **$60.**

Walnut clock shelf with carved dog head and roundels, 13″ wide, 6″ deep, 14″ high. In Illinois, **$130.**

Walnut ebonized wall shelf with pewter elk head, 10″ wide, 6″ deep, 15″ high. In Illinois, **$200.**

Walnut corner wall shelf cut off from standing what-not, 28″ wide, 31″ high, 19″ deep, graduates to 12″ deep at top shelf. In Indiana, **$75.**

Brass easel frame, 8″ wide, 11″ high. In Iowa, **$42.**

Walnut corner shelf, 12″ wide, 8″ deep, 23″ high. In Iowa, **$80.**

Wall shelf, stained dark, incised lines; 18" wide, 6" deep, 26" high. In Arkansas, **$225.** Left to right, top to bottom: Royal Bayreuth rose tapestry pitcher, 4" high, **$200.** Rainbow mother-of-pearl, herringbone ewer, 6" high, **$800.** Unmarked R. S. Prussia creamer, 4" high, **$125.** Royal Bayreuth rose tapestry powder jar with unusual orange roses, 4" diameter, 3" high, **$300.** Unmarked pin try attributed to Wave Crest, 4" diameter, 3" high, **$150.** Mt. Washington egg-shaped sugar shaker, 5" high, **$300.** Crown Milano sugar shaker, 4" diameter, 3" high; salt and pepper shakers, 3" diameter, 2" high; **$400** the set.

Double liner gold frame with flowers painted on front of glass insert, 15" wide, 17" high. In Pennsylvania, **$145.**

Empty walnut shadow box, 23" wide, 8" deep, 32" high. In Illinois, **$325.**

Oak and gold multilinear frame with hand-painted platter, signed E. G. Bryan '94; 28″ wide, 32″ high. In Texas, **$300.**

Multilinear gold frame, 32″ wide, 38″ high. In Texas, **$300.**

Walnut and gold multilinear frame with fruit reverse painting on back of glass insert, 15″ wide, 13″ high. In Pennsylvania, **$80.**

Plaster of Paris gold frame, 17″ wide, 29″ high. In Pennsylvania, **$250.**

Bronze Phoenix oil lamp made by Bradley and Hubbard, 1880 patent date; 39″ high. In Illinois, **$2,800.**

Walnut crisscross picture frame with carved leaves at the corners. In Illinois, **$150.**

Brass oil lamp with filigree over opaque glass shade, 27″ high. In Illinois, **$450.**

Brass organ lamp that can be raised and lowered. with floral globe. In Illinois, **$750.**

Three-piece mantel garniture set with center clock and two girandoles (candelabras), English. Clock, 17″ wide, 7″ deep, 19″ high. Candleholders, 22″ high. In Illinois, **$1,250** the set.

Rosewood clock by James Smith, Grantown; 19″ wide base, 9″ deep, 24″ high. In Texas, **$1,250.**

Walnut shelf clock with Statue of Liberty on door and Columbia head near crest, made by the Ingraham Company, Bristol, Connecticut; 14½″ wide, 4½″ deep, 25″ high. In Pennsylvania, **$225.**

Walnut shelf clock with brass decorations, manufactured by Welch of Bristol, Connecticut; 16″ wide, 7″ deep, 25″ high. In Texas, **$300**. Walnut Eastlake shelf, 24″ wide, 6″ deep, 11″ high. **$110**.

Walnut shelf clock made by the Gilbert Clock Company, Winsted, Connecticut; 13″ wide, 5″ deep, 20″ high. In Illinois, **$225**.

Walnut shelf clock with Columbia head, 12″ wide, 4″ deep, 20″ high. In Pennsylvania, **$225**.

Walnut shelf clock, 14″ wide, 22″ high. In Indiana, **$250**.

Cast iron shelf clock with brass plaque that indicates it was a wedding gift in 1901. In Texas, **$200.**

Walnut Seth Thomas wall clock, 13″ wide, 4″ deep, 31″ high. In Iowa, **$750.**

Walnut wall clock with brass face, 13″ wide, 7″ deep, 39″ high. In Iowa, **$2,500.**

Walnut Seth Thomas wall clock, 14″ wide, 7″ deep, 48″ high. In Iowa, **$510.**

Mahogany long case clock (now called grandfather clock) with brass weights on brass cables, inlay, and removable top, made by J. Smith & Sons, St. John's Sqr., Clerkenwell, London, and presented as a gift to a commissioner of the 1893 Columbian Exposition, Chicago. In Indiana, **$5,000.**

Birdcage that resembles house, 23″ wide, 15″ deep, 19″ high. In Wisconsin, **$85.**

Base of table with legs formed from carved birds standing on rams' heads, 27″ high legs.

Rogers' grouping, entitled "Coming to the Parson," 1870; 17″ wide, 22″ high. In Illinois, **$850.**

Album holder with drawer for additional pictures, handmade, partly from cigar boxes; 8″ wide, 7″ deep, 11″ high. In Iowa, **$75.**

Game bird that hangs upside down on walnut sideboard, 11″ wide, 14″ high.

Carved cherub on walnut oval mirror frame, 15″ high from toe to fingertip.

Carved head of boy on walnut desk, 3″ wide, 5″ high.

Carved figure of child on base of walnut table, 13″ high.

Applied carved decoration on headboard of walnut bed, 20″ high.

Applied carved decoration on footboard of walnut bed, 10″ wide, 11″ high.

Pot metal insert plaque in circular medallion frame on walnut sideboard, 11″ diameter.

❧ 11 ❧
Decorating in the Victorian Style

Telephone callers from many states inquire, "My wife likes to make needlepoint. Would it be acceptable to use it to upholster Victorian chairs? What colors were predominant in the 1800s? What fabrics were popular for draperies and upholstery?"

Victoriana is as multifaceted as a cut gem. Because Queen Victoria reigned for sixty-three years, styles did not remain static. But while Victoriana incorporated numerous styles, there were dominant trends.

Females were encouraged to express creativity through embroidery, art, and needlepoint. A girl bent her head over an outline stamped on a fabric to create a petit-point picture for a fire screen or a seat cover. It required the daintiest of stitches over one vertical and one horizontal canvas thread. While the stitch was repetitious, the different colors of threads selected created red roses with green leaves or the feathers and shape of birds. Needlepoint embroidery in worsted threads and silks also was attractive. Silk patchwork added bright touches to home decor. A Victorian woman was proud when the upholsterer brought back a sofa and chairs that showed off her artistry with a needle. When a skilled hand executes such work today, it does indeed fit into a restored Victorian setting.

Horsehair cloth, woven from strands from the mane and tail of horses, formed a stiff, slippery upholstery material that was used widely in the nineteenth century. Usually linen threads were included in the weave. While black was the main color, other colors appeared too, and even a tiny print was available. It is possible to purchase haircloth today. Any plush, a fabric with a thick, soft pile such as plain velvet, is associated with the parlor of the past, especially after horsehair was labeled old fashioned in the 1870s. Other fabrics included brocatelle (a heavy figured cloth usually made of silk and linen) and glossy-faced satins (including satin damask). Damask, a durable, reversible, lustrous fabric with a figured weave, served well for table linens and upholstery. An embroidered type was available also.

Favorite colors between 1840 and 1865 included red, black, dark brown, green, delicate pink, soft blue, and a variety of purples. In 1859, a purplish red shade called magenta was introduced. Frames were left exposed on parlor suites. While coils were invented in the 1700s, it was not until the mid-1800s that these helix springs were inexpensively produced to add a bouncy comfort to seats. Padding choices included feathers, down, straw, or animal hair. The latter sometimes pricked through its fabric cover.

The color accents changed from time to time. After all, when the nineteenth century was new, people still concocted their own paints. Much as a money-saving housewife throws together leftovers to create a meal, people experimented with combining milk, eggs, coffee grounds, or other ingredients as they stirred up a batch of paint. The results were not consistent. As the 1800s began, it was possible to buy a mix-it-yourself preparation, but not until 1867 was a prepared, ready-to-use paint marketed. It was both low priced and easy to use. In the first half of the 1800s, white woodwork was modish. Walls were frequently a pastel blue or green or pale red. As the years progressed, the colors gradually deepened.

Windows had about as many inner and outer garments as a lady wore. The layered look was achieved with a drapery covering the upper part of the window, hung over curtains that might in turn cover shades or blinds. A cornice was hung atop the windows to hide the rods and curtain endings. Heavy side draperies were tied back with tasseled silk cords. Brocade, a rich cloth with a raised design of velvet, silk, silver, or gold woven into it, was considered rich in appearance for draperies. Other popular choices included soft, shiny silk, fine yet rather stiff silk taffeta, or moiré, a watered or wavy lustrous pattern on cloth such as silk.

It seemed as though everything had to be covered with fabric. The piano, tables, stands, and the sofa all were draped. A center table usually held a large Bible and was the site of the family prayers. Hanging baskets of flowers and potted plants occupied sunny areas. Real vines served as wall festoons or were trained to trail around pictures that hung from the molding with visible cords.

Carpets had large floral and geometric patterns. Power loom and mass production brought these floor coverings into the reach of the middle class. Carpets whose fibers were dyed and deeply infused with color before they were factory woven were referred to as ingrained. Axminster looms wove fine, knotted-pile carpets in the same manner that handmade oriental rugs are made. Wilton looms, using a jacquard attachment, were able to produce a durable carpet more economically. Soon carpet was found in many homes. Patterns and color combinations varied, but decorators suggested that dark hues made a room appear larger.

Victorians liked disguises. Molded dolphins became candleholders, ceramic hands were ring holders, and miniature shoes served as snuff boxes or pincushions. When steam-powered presses made it possible for manufacturers to produce wallpaper in colors, homeowners wanted the paper to represent something it wasn't. Some rolls looked like wainscoting, dado, or cornices to add architectural interests to plain rooms. Heavy textures sometimes had an embossed, leathery appearance. Fabric was imitated so that walls appeared to be clothed with damask or silk. Other walls wore paper with stripes and large naturalistic flowers.

The mid- to late-Victorian parlor was cluttered enough to make a magpie chirp with glee. Étagères held souvenirs, photographs, and china. A mantel and overmantel were crowded with bric-a-brac. By the 1880s, the room seemed as overcrowded as a toy store at Christmastime. Fragile stands and chairs competed with stocky patent rockers for attention. By the 1890s, stained glass windows were commercially produced and promptly placed in halls, bathrooms, and stairways.

Lace curtains and velvet plush upholstery were key decorating elements in the later 1800s. Charles Lock(e) Eastlake, the English architect who disliked fussy lines in furniture had a distaste for cornices and fringes, which he disdainfully referred to as ravelings. He advocated simple styles, and others joined him in promoting plainer window treatments. As a result, the style switched to curtains and draperies hung on exposed, turned rods by means of brass rings. Fringe on furniture upholstery was taboo also.

In the 1870s, hardwood floors, customarily of oak, were exposed, and the wealthy bought genuine, hand-tied Oriental rugs while the bourgeoisie was content with factory imitations. Country homes sometimes chose homemade hooked or braided rugs for their floors.

Gradually, fashion dictated that woodwork should not be painted. Instead, it was given a finish called French polish that was actually a varnish. Wall colors deepened and more neutral tones emerged. If wallpaper was applied, floral patterns tended to have an abstract rather than realistic appearance.

As the 1870s ended, articles in magazines urged families to reject the parlor for a living room. Why save the best for occasional company? The loved ones in the family circle were more important than guests and should enjoy the top accommodations the home had to offer. When oldsters clung to the traditional parlor idea as tenaciously as a hull to a walnut, writers urged newlyweds to loosen up and set a fresh trend. Let the home be for the family to have and to hold. A room could only become a functioning part of the house if it was used consistently.

Remember, many members of the emerging middle class tried to be fashionable while the affluent families flaunted their wealth by lavishly showing off their possessions. Naturally there would be a vast difference between the home furnishings of these two classes. Therefore, it is important to realize that these are rough approximations only. If you are redoing a Victorian home, visit one in your area. Library books are available that tell about restored sites that are open to the public. These are only suggestions. Incorporate your own ideas as you emulate the Victorian era. It's exciting to hunt for accessory items and to create an interior that complements your personality. As the women of the nineteenth century liked to say in the embroidered words they framed, "Home is where the heart is" or "Home sweet home." They also appreciated the statement, "Bless this house" — a phrase, we believe, is a fitting way to conclude this book.

✎ Glossary ✎

Applied An ornamentation crafted separately and attached to a piece of furniture.

Apron A piece used as a "connecting skirt" in chairs, cabinets, and tables. It may be used as a structural aid or to hide the construction. The apron is found between the legs of cabinets, cupboards, and chests. In a table, it is beneath the top, connecting the legs. In a chair, it is the portion under the seat. Not all tables and chairs have an apron.

Arched molding A half-round convex strip used for trim.

Armoire A large cupboard or wardrobe of the type originally used in the Middle Ages to store armor.

Atlantes A male figure that serves as a supporting column.

Bail handle A drawer pull with a brass half-loop pendant fastened to a back plate.

Balloon back A chair back shaped something like a hot air balloon.

Beading A thin strip of molding that resembles small beads in a continuous line.

Bevel A slanted edge on a board or sheet of glass.

Breakfront Used on some bookcases, desks, wardrobes, and sideboards. The straight lines of the front are broken by a lower vertical portion that juts out.

Broken pediment A top ornament that does not meet completely at the apex (highest point).

Bureau washstand A small, three-drawer chest used to hold a wash bowl and pitcher. Some have a retractable towel bar holder or towel bar ends.

Burl An abnormal, humped growth on some trees. It can be sliced thin to make decorative veneers.

Cabriole leg A leg with a double curve. It bulges at the knee and bends in and out again at the ankle.

Cane Long, narrow strips of rattan used for weaving chair seats and backs.

Canopy The framework on top of tall posts of a bed (resembles a roof over the bed). Also called a tester.

Caryatid A female figure that serves as a supporting column.

Case piece The box-like structure that forms the outside of a cabinet, desk, chest of drawers, etc.

Chamfer An edge or corner cut off at a slant.

Cheval glass A full-length mirror that swings from vertical posts. Its small counterpart, which sits on a table or chest, may include a drawer as well as the mirror.

Circa or c About or around a certain date.

Circular molding An ornamental strip applied or carved on furniture in a circular or oval contour. It may be incised or raised.

Commode A washstand with an enclosed cupboard.

Composition A plaster of Paris, resin, sizing, and water mixture molded to resemble carving.

Corner stile The upright at the corner of a piece of furniture.

Cornice The top horizontal molding on some articles of furniture.

Crest or cresting The ornamental top of a pediment, chair, or sofa back.

Curule legs Rounded legs that form an X shape and are similar to a Roman style.

Cylinder A quarter-round rolling top on a desk or secretary front.

Cyma A double curve, as in a cabriole leg.

Davenport A small writing desk used during the 1800s. The sloping top lifts up so articles can be stored in the compartment beneath, and usually the drawers pull out sideways instead of toward the front.

Demi-arm The supporting brace that joins a chair back and seat. Also called a hip rest.

Drop front *See* Fall front.

Ebony and gilt drops Pear-shaped pendants attached to a round brass plate. Term found in catalogs of the 1800s for drawer pulls; now called "teardrops."

Eclectic Mixture of styles.

Escutcheon A fitting around a keyhole. Often made of brass or wood, it may be inset or applied.

Fall front A type of desk with a hinged lid that drops down to form a writing surface.

Finger grip A groove cut in the lower edge of a drawer front to use in place of a handle or knob.

Finger roll Continuous concave molding cut into the frame of a chair or sofa.

Finial A turned, carved, or cast end ornament of a clock, table, bedstead post, or pediment.

Flush Level with the surrounding surface.

Fret or fretwork An ornamental border, perforated or cut in low relief.

Gallery A raised railing or rim of wood or metal around the top of a desk, table, sideboard, etc.

Geometric A pattern made by interlacing circles, triangles, squares, and similar designs.

Hip rest *See* Demi-arm.

Incise Design cut into or engraved in the surface.

Inlay Forming designs by inserting into wood contrasting colors, grains, and textures of wood, metal, shells, or ivory.

Inset pilaster An artificial, decorative pillar inserted on a flat surface, most frequently at the front corners of a case piece.

Laminated Layers of wood glued together with the grain of each succeeding layer at a right angle to the ones before; provides strength.

Louis XV French style named for the ruler who reigned from 1717-1774. Graceful curves and elliptical shapes. Dainty. Cabriole leg. Floral and fruit carvings.

Molding A continuous ornamental edging applied to or carved in furniture.

Ogee A molding with a double continuous curve; S shaped.

Panel A square or rectangular board held in place by a grooved framework. It can be beneath the framework, flush with it, or above it.

Pediment An ornamental top on a piece of furniture.

Pendant finial A downward finial.

Pie crust A table's decorative edge that resembles the pinched rim on a pie's crust.

Pierced carving Open-work carving.

Pier glass or mirror A tall, narrow mirror often hung between two long windows, either extending to the floor or with a console table beneath it.

Pilaster A decorative artificial pillar with no structural strength, set against a background. Often it is half-round or rectangular.

Projection front A top that extends over the rest of the piece as a projecting top drawer overhangs the drawers beneath.

Pull brackets The slides located on each side of a desk or secretary that pull out to support the dropped-down writing surface.

Pull slides *See* Pull brackets.

Raised panel A panel that projects slightly above the surrounding surface and is often molded.

Renaissance Revival of interest in ancient Greek and Roman culture. Elaborate carving. Heavy, imposing, ornamental furniture. Circa 1850-1885.

Ring molding A circular ornamental edging applied to or carved in furniture.

Rococo An elaborate style of decoration that employed natural objects such as shells, fruits, flowers, leaves, and nuts, in an elaborate fashion.

Rounded end The curved rather than straight corner of case pieces.

Rung The simple or turned cross piece that connects cabinet, chair, or table legs near the bottom. A runner or stretcher.

Runner Another name for the rocker on a rocking chair; a guide strip to support a drawer; slides on which the drop fronts on desks are supported.

Scalloped A series of curves derived from a shell shape that form an ornamental edge.

Serpentine Resembling the outline of a snake in motion; a snake-like curve that is convex at the center and ends and concave between.

Skirt *See* Apron.

Slant front A hinged lid on a desk that drops down to form a writing surface.

Slat A horizontal crossbar in chair backs.

Splat The center upright in a chair back.

Spool turning Resembling buttons, knobs, balls, or like objects strung together.

Spoon carving Hollowed-out surface designs resembling the bowl of a spoon.

Stile The upright of a frame or panel in furniture. *See* Corner stile.

Stretcher *See* Rung.

Teapoy Small table for tea service (archaic term).

Tester *See* Canopy.

Tilt-top A table hinged to the top of a center post so that it can be tipped to a vertical position.

Turning Shaping wood on a lathe with chisels; a piece shaped by turning.

Urn A decorative vase with a base used as a finial.

Whatnot A tier of shelves connected by turned posts and used to display knick-knacks.

❧ Bibliography ❧

Aronson, Joseph. *Encyclopedia of Furniture*. New York, N.Y.: Crown Publishers, Inc., 1965.

Bradford, Ernle. *Dictionary of Antiques*. London, England: The English Universities Press Ltd., 1963.

Dubrow, Eileen and Richard. *American Furniture of the 19th Century, 1840-1880*. Exton, Pennsylvania: Schiffer Publishing Ltd., 1983.

Grotz, George. *The New Antiques*. Garden City, N.Y.: Doubleday & Company, 1964.

McClinton, Katherine Morrison. *Collecting American Victorian Antiques*. New York: Charles Scribner's Sons, 1966.

Miller, Robert W. *Clock Guide No. 2*. Des Moines, Iowa: Wallace-Homestead Book Company, 1976.

Norbury, James. *The World of Victoriana*. London, New York, Sidney, Toronto: Hamlyn, 1972.

Oliver, J.L. *The Development and Structure of the Furniture Industry*. Oxford, London, Edinburgh, New York, Toronto, Paris, Braunschweig: Pergamon Press, 1966.

Ormsbee, Thomas H. *Field Guide to American Victorian Furniture*. Boston, Mass.: Little, Brown and Company, 1952.

Otto, Celia Jackson. *American Furniture of the Nineteenth Century*. New York: The Viking Press, 1965.

Ransom, Frank Edward. *The City Built on Wood, a History of the Furniture Industry in Grand Rapids, Michigan*. Ann Arbor, Michigan: Edwards Bros., Inc., 1955.

Revi, Albert Christian, Ed. and the staff of "Spinning Wheel Magazine." *The Spinning Wheel's Complete Book of Antiques*. New York: Grosset & Dunlap, 1972.

Swartz, Marvin D., Edward J. Stanek, and Douglas K. True. *The Furniture of John Henry Belter and the Rococo Revival*. New York: E.P. Dutton, 1981.

Shull, Thelma. *Victorian Antiques*. Rutland, Vermont: Charles E. Tuttle Company, 1963.

Swedberg, Robert and Harriett. *Victorian Furniture Styles and Prices, Book I Revised*. West Des Moines, Iowa: Wallace-Homestead Book Co., 1984.

Swedberg, Robert and Harriett. *Victorian Furniture Styles and Prices, Book 11 Revised*. Des Moines, Iowa: Wallace-Homestead Book Co., 1983.

Symonds, R. W., and B. B. Whineray. *Victorian Furniture*. London: Country Life Limited, 1962.

Tracy, Berry B., Marilyn Johnson, Marvin D. Schwartz, and Suzanne Boorsch. *19th Century America: Furniture and Other Decorative Arts*. New York: Metropolitan Museum of Art, 1970.

Yates, Raymond F. and Marguerite W. *Victorian Antiques*. New York: Gramercy Publishing Company, 1949. (Harper and Row published originally.)

Periodicals

National Association of Watch and Clock Collectors, Inc., A Supplement to the *Bulletin. Eli Terry — Dreamer, Artisan, and Clockmaker* (Summer, 1965).

Downs, Joseph. "John Henry Belter and Company." *Antiques*, 166-168: (September, 1948).

Reference Works

The World Book Encyclopedia. Chicago: Field Enterprises Educational Corporation, 1966.

❧ Index ❧

❧ About the Authors ❧

When Bob and Harriett Swedberg research and write books, they travel thousands of miles. They meet many fine people who share their interest in preserving heritage articles for future generations. While they enjoy visiting museums, they do not include museum pieces in their books. The Swedbergs photograph only articles that are actually available to the public to purchase or are in the possession of people who have secured them to preserve and collect. To date, this couple has written books on oak, country furniture, wicker, Victorian, and advertising, as well as on refinishing and repairing antiques. They are available as speakers and enjoy teaching about America's heritage through antiques classes.